VINTAGE WISCONSIN GARDENS

GARDENS
A HISTORY OF HOME GARDENING

VINTAGE WISCONSIN GARDENS

A HISTORY OF HOME GARDENING

LEE SOMERVILLE

foreword by Arnold R. Alanen

WISCONSIN HISTORICAL SOCIETY PRESS

Published by the Wisconsin Historical Society Press
Publishers since 1855

© 2011 by the State Historical Society of Wisconsin

For permission to reuse material from *Vintage Wisconsin Gardens: A History of Home Gardening*, 978-0-87020-475-3, please access www.copyright.com or contact the Copyright Clearance Center, Inc. (CCC), 222 Rosewood Drive, Danvers, MA 01923, 978-750-8400. CCC is a not-for-profit organization that provides licenses and registration for a variety of users.

wisconsin**history**.org

Photographs identified with WHi or WHS are from the Society's collections; address requests to reproduce these photos to the Visual Materials Archivist at the Wisconsin Historical Society, 816 State Street, Madison, WI 53706.
Back cover: WHi Image ID 27008
Frontmatter photo credits: page v: Cadwell & Jones, *1900 Catalogue of Seeds and Agricultural Implements*; page vi: *Vick's Monthly Magazine*, November 1878; page viii: *Vick's Monthly Magazine*, February 1879; page xii: *Vick's Monthly Magazine*, June 1882; pages xiv–xx: illustrations adapted from *Vick's Monthly Magazine*, June 1879; page xvi: *Vick's Monthly Magazine*, November 1879.

Printed in the United States of America
Designed by Steve Biel

15 14 13 12 11   1 2 3 4 5

Library of Congress Cataloging-in-Publication Data

Somerville, Lee.
    Vintage Wisconsin gardens : a history of home gardening / Lee Somerville ; foreword by Arnold R. Alanen.
        p. cm.
    Includes bibliographical references and index.
    ISBN 978-0-87020-475-3 (pbk. : alk. paper) 1. Gardening—Wisconsin—History. 2. Gardens—Wisconsin—History. I. Title.
    SB451.34.W6S66 2011
    635.909775—dc22
                                2011001830

∞ The paper used in this publication meets the minimum requirements of the American National Standard for Information Sciences—Permanence of Paper for Printed Library Materials, ANSI Z39.48–1992.

Dedicated to Wisconsin gardeners,
past, present, and future

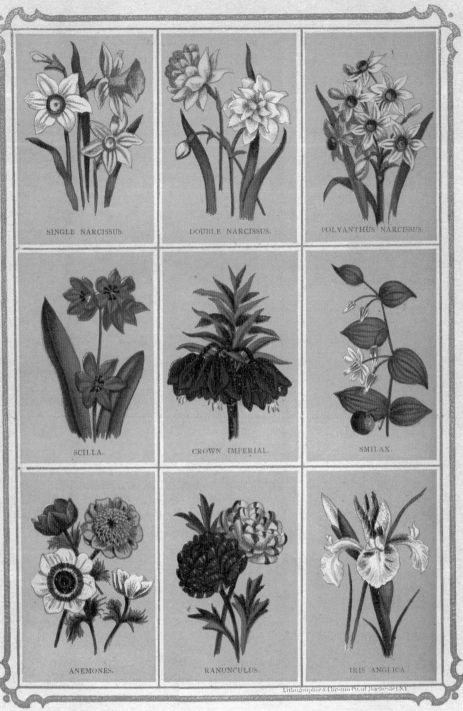

SINGLE NARCISSUS. DOUBLE NARCISSUS. POLYANTHUS NARCISSUS.

SCILLA. CROWN IMPERIAL. SMILAX.

ANEMONES. RANUNCULUS. IRIS ANGLICA.

Lithographic & Chromo Co. of Rochester N.Y.

Painted For Vick's Monthly.

Contents

FOREWORD ix

ACKNOWLEDGMENTS xi

INTRODUCTION xiii

1 Changing Ideals in Nineteenth-Century American Vernacular Gardens 1

2 From Farmstead to Village 23

3 The Pleasures and Benefits of Amateur Horticulture 43

4 Beautifying the Home Grounds 59

5 Graceful Vines and Sweet Wild Roses: Recommended Plants 101

6 In the Wisconsin Garden— Yesterday and Today 125

APPENDIX: RECOMMENDED VARIETIES 141

NOTES 151

SELECTED BIBLIOGRAPHY 163

INDEX 169

Foreword

Any observant person who travels throughout present-day Wisconsin cannot help but notice that well-tended, orderly, and often imaginative gardens, yards, and lawns appear in abundance throughout the state. Whether in rural, suburban, or urban areas, many Wisconsin residents take a strong interest in creating, making, and maintaining the outdoor spaces that serve as settings for their homes and farmsteads.

The origins of these present-day residential spaces, which collectively form a major portion of the state's overall cultural landscape, may be traced back to the mid-nineteenth century—a time when some areas of Wisconsin began to undergo the transition from frontier conditions to a more domesticated and "civilized" environment. Granted, the changes did not occur overnight, even as Wisconsin achieved statehood in 1848 and its population expanded from 31,000 in 1840 to 776,000 in 1860. During this twenty-year period Wisconsin's American- and foreign-born residents mined ore, developed townsites, and cleared land for agricultural purposes. Following the end of the Civil War in 1865, the foundation for Wisconsin's quintessential dairy farm landscape began to emerge, and its towns and cities attracted increasing numbers of inhabitants. By 1920, when the population total exceeded 2.6 million people, the state's settlement framework was in place, and Wisconsin was fully integrated into all facets of national life and activity. It is the period described above, from the 1840s to 1930, that Lee Somerville covers in *Vintage Wisconsin Gardens: A History of Home Gardening*.

Unlike the majority of American garden history books, which focus on formal and "high style" examples, this volume features vernacular gardens—the outdoor spaces that Wisconsinites themselves created for their own use and enjoyment. For the most part, these people did not have access to a professional landscape designer, or the monetary resources to hire one; however, there was an organization that could provide them with free garden-related advice: the Wisconsin State Horticultural Society, formed during the mid-nineteenth century. Of special importance to people who wished to enhance their garden knowledge were the proceedings that appeared after each WSHS annual meeting, and which members received from 1869 to 1928. It is the WSHS literature that Lee has thoroughly reviewed, classified, and summarized in developing this account of Wisconsin's residential gardens and horticultural practices.

Another important feature of *Vintage Wisconsin Gardens* is the light it shines on the essential role that women played in creating and nurturing gardens, a theme that has only relatively recently been pursued by scholars. In 1984 Annette Kolodny published a pathbreaking book—*The Land Before Her: Fantasy and Experience of the American Frontiers, 1630–1860*—which spelled out differences between male and female perceptions of the nation's pioneer landscapes. While men viewed the virginal land as something to conquer and exploit, women "claimed the frontiers as a potential sanctuary for an idealized domesticity." The feminine wish, as related by Kolodny, was to provide "a home and a familial human community within a cultivated garden."[1] A similar but somewhat more poetic message, prominently cited in *Vintage Wisconsin Gardens*, was offered by Mrs. D. Huntley of Appleton in 1873: "Her [Wisconsin's] own peculiar climate shall yield its own peculiar fruit, and beautiful homes, with splendid trees and clustering vines, and fragrant flowers shall everywhere adorn her prairies and her woodlands."[2]

The book concludes with two chapters that will prove especially useful to anyone involved in or contemplating the restoration, development, or interpretation of a period garden in Wisconsin. After offering a consolidated listing of plants recommended by the WSHS for a successful garden, the subsequent chapter discusses steps for implementation. Although implementation may appear challenging, Lee provides a reasonable and clearly understandable set of guidelines to take one through the process. For those who still feel intimidated or overwhelmed by this task, Lee offers reassuring words: any historical garden, she writes, is a "representation" of the past that "can never be entirely accurate."

Vintage Wisconsin Gardens reflects Lee's lifetime of horticultural experience, coupled with several years of research and writing. Born and raised in England—a country whose citizens are noted for their love of gardens and gardening—Lee brought her knowledge and interests to Wisconsin, where she successfully adapted them to a different plant palette and a harsher climate. In addition, she gained significant hands-on experience as a historical interpreter and gardener at Heritage Hill State Historical Park in Green Bay and at Old World Wisconsin in Eagle. Those of us who call Wisconsin home are indebted to Lee for devoting her skill, time, and energy to the task of cultivating a greater understanding of our state's garden heritage.

Arnold R. Alanen, professor emeritus,
Department of Landscape Architecture, University of Wisconsin–Madison

Acknowledgments

This undertaking is the fulfillment of a goal I have had for many years: to provide a useful garden history for Wisconsin gardeners, especially those who work at historic sites. I am indebted to all those who helped me shape my research and encouraged my vision.

There are too many to list by name, but the following were especially supportive:

Professors Arnold R. Alanen, Janet C. Gilmore, and Anna V. Andrzejewski, who guided me through my research while I was a graduate student in the Department of Landscape Architecture at the University of Wisconsin–Madison.

The volunteers and staff of Heritage Hill State Historical Park in Green Bay and Old World Wisconsin in Eagle, who graciously allowed me to wander through their sites, buildings, and archives.

The Wisconsin Master Gardener Association, especially the members of my home Door County group, and those who garden at the many historic sites throughout the state.

My editor, Laura Kearney, who patiently corrected my convoluted syntax and grammar, shortened my sentences, and made me find answers to questions I had been avoiding. Mike Nemer, who expertly shepherded the book through the production process and attended to the details. And the book's designer Steve Biel, who used his gardener's eye to integrate the text and the photographs into such colorful harmony.

Last, though certainly not least, my family and many friends, including my children, Sara and Patrick, and their spouses; my sisters, Sheila and Mary; and Kris, Linda, and Jon.

Introduction

This book is the result of my long-standing interest in gardens and gardening. I've pulled weeds, planted flowers, and grown herbs in many gardens, following in my mother's and grandmother's footsteps. In 1976, when I first came to live in Wisconsin, I was shocked at the harshness of the climate and doubted I would ever be comfortable here, let alone able to nurture a garden. But I learned to adapt, just like the nineteenth-century immigrants who successfully established their homes, gardens, and communities in this unfamiliar region.

I was quickly captivated by Wisconsin's unique settlement history and was fortunate to be able to combine my areas of interest when I began volunteering as a historical interpreter and gardener at Heritage Hill State Historical Park in Green Bay. Through theme areas, each containing several historic structures, this fifty-acre living history site portrays the events and people that shaped Green Bay and northeastern Wisconsin over three hundred years. Over time I found myself more and more involved in the history of the gardens surrounding the homes, and began a quest to discover how they were originally planned and planted. The staff and volunteers had noticed that visitors to the park were increasingly interested in what was growing in the gardens and why, and we wanted to be able to answer their questions accurately. We also realized that the landscape around the buildings should be incorporated into the existing interpretive plans that told the stories of the lives and interests of the people who settled and lived in northeastern Wisconsin.

At most historic sites, the enormous expenditure of time and funding needed to preserve, maintain, furnish, and interpret the interior and exterior of important structures tends to take precedence over the landscape. Often, interested, knowledgeable, and enthusiastic local gardeners are encouraged to develop and maintain the surrounding gardens, but they are seldom given specific guidelines, and resources (and funding) for research are not generally readily available. Even with the recent increased interest in heirloom seeds and plants—and, indeed, in gardening and garden history—it is not easy to unearth the detail needed to portray the narrative of a specific garden. Ideally, the landscape should supplement and enhance the interpretation of a historic building by

ASTER

further demonstrating the cultural traditions and ethnic history of earlier times. With the rising interest in home gardening and the ever-increasing availability of heirloom varieties of seeds and plants, historic sites have not only an opportunity but perhaps a responsibility to provide visitors with accurate representations of the gardens framing their buildings.

As I became more involved with the gardens and the groups maintaining them, I found myself asking more questions than my gardening books could answer about the form and composition of area historic gardens. Existing works on American garden history mainly focused on the works of well-known landscape architects and their high-style, designed estates along the eastern seaboard, rather than the everyday, or vernacular, gardens of ordinary people.

While the late nineteenth century produced increasing amounts of garden literature, both in book and magazine format, these publications, for the most part, originated along the eastern seaboard. What I was looking for were primary and secondary regional and local resources that would provide Wisconsin homeowners, historic site administrators, and gardeners with the information they needed to establish or reconstruct an accurate representation of a late-nineteenth- or early-twentieth-century garden. I was sure it was available if I just knew where to look, and eventually I realized that I needed to endeavor to answer my questions through an academic approach.

To that end, I applied and was accepted into the master's program of the Department of Landscape Architecture at UW–Madison in the fall of 2004. I was encouraged by an extremely supportive group of faculty members to proceed with my study, which was to locate, consolidate, and document the horticultural and garden literature written specifically for Wisconsin homeowners in the late nineteenth and early twentieth centuries. I wanted to provide an easily accessible baseline for all who are interested in Wisconsin garden history research; additionally, I expected that this research would determine whether national garden history publications were valid at the regional level.

The major questions I asked were, first, what were the primary sources of garden information for Wisconsin homeowners during the mid- to late nineteenth and early twentieth centuries, and how successfully were they

BALSAM

❧ WHAT IS A VERNACULAR GARDEN? ❧

The term *garden*, from the Latin *gardinus*, shares its roots with the term *yard*, and the two words are often used interchangeably in the United States. However, the original meaning of *garden* was "enclosed area."[1] The meaning of the term *vernacular* is more complicated. Originally the Latin word *verna* meant "home-born slave," implying someone who belonged to a house. The term *vernacular* later came to mean a "way of speaking that is tied to or characteristic of a particular region."[2] From this came the current usage of "everyday" or "ordinary."

In historic preservation terminology, the phrase *vernacular architecture* was originally used as a catchall to describe everyday, nonarchitecturally designed buildings. Recently, however, architectural historians have expanded this definition, stating that "vernacular architecture is not just a type of architecture, but also an approach to architectural studies that emphasizes the intimate relationships between everyday objects

and culture, between ordinary buildings and people."[3] In the same sense, the vernacular garden is not only the area surrounding a vernacular home but is also interconnected to and a reflection of the occupants of that home. The changing appearance and function of the house and garden over time can be further defined as the result of the interactive relationship between people and their home landscape. The vernacular garden is many layered, retaining incompletely erased remnants of earlier occupancy in its form and composition.

NOTES

1. *Oxford English Dictionary*, 2nd ed., s.v. "garden."

2. Thomas Carter and Elizabeth Collins Cromley, *Invitation to Vernacular Architecture: A Guide to the Study of Ordinary Buildings and Landscapes* (Knoxville: University of Tennessee Press, 2005), xv.

3. Ibid.

disseminated throughout the state? Second, what were the major recommendations and guidelines for the development and maintenance of rural and urban vernacular gardens, and how did they change over the time span? And third, can the completed analysis provide a timeline for changes in Wisconsin home gardens, and, if so, is there a relationship between regional and national trends during that same period? In other words, is there a model, or models, that could be used to create or restore a "typical" Wisconsin garden to a particular time period or a particular location? To aid in my research I focused on a specific time period—that of the late nineteenth and early twentieth centuries—but this by no means implies that the form and composition of mid-twentieth-century gardens is not an equally interesting topic.

PAINTED FOR VICKS MONTHLY

FUCHSIAS.

DIANTHUS

Once I had formulated and organized my research, I began to look at resources and fairly quickly came across a wide selection of little-known primary information and published literature on Wisconsin gardens. I gathered and consolidated it all, finding much of it extremely valuable, some quite surprising, and all of it interesting.

The most helpful was the collected published proceedings of the annual meetings of the Wisconsin State Horticultural Society (WSHS). Based in Madison, the WSHS originated as a special-interest fruit-growers group under the broader umbrella organization of the Wisconsin State Agricultural Society during the 1850s and forged its own constitution in 1865. The foremost mission of the society was to promote the development of orchards, with a secondary stated goal of advancing horticultural knowledge and practice throughout the state. In spite of its comparatively small membership and homogeneous ethnicity, its publications are still the best source for the ideas and ideals of horticultural practice that were predominant in Wisconsin during this time period.[1]

The proceedings of the annual meetings were distributed to all society members, in book form, between 1869 and 1928. Initially titled *Transactions of the Wisconsin State Horticultural Society*, it was renamed the *Annual Report of the Wisconsin State Horticultural Society* in 1890. Each volume contained a full transcript of the papers, presentations, discussions, and business meetings held at the annual and, later, biennial meetings of the previous year. Sometimes papers were also submitted in written form to the WSHS secretary for inclusion. Two society journals, *The Wisconsin Horticulturist* (1896–1903) and *Wisconsin Horticulture* (1910–1967), supplemented the annual report. These journals, especially *Wisconsin Horticulture*, offered an informal exchange of information between members and the society's officers through question-and-answer segments, editorials, opinions, and photographs.[2]

I began by selecting all presentations, articles, and reports related to home horticulture from the fifty-nine years' worth of *Transactions* and *Annual Reports* and in all issues of *The Wisconsin Horticulturist* and *Wisconsin Horticulture*. I copied, subdivided, and analyzed the 450 presentations and articles I found. The first and largest group consisted of about 300

MIGNONETTE

presentations and articles that specifically addressed methods of "improving," "beautifying," or "ornamenting" the home grounds. A review of these presentations forms the basis of this book.

Buried within a common theme of civic, family, and personal improvement through horticulture is a thread that deserves attention: the role of women in the home and garden, and, by implication, in society. Women often presented at the annual meetings, and their voices resonate—tentatively during the first years of society operation, but with increasing confidence and assurance. What they had to say is significant and relevant, and I have included several of their remarks, either as epigraphs or within the text of this book. Their changing role within the society is discussed in more detail in chapter 3, as are the civic improvement objectives they were promoting.

PANSY

While personal, family, and civic topics are not directly related to the improvement of home grounds, they are relevant because they reveal the issues WSHS members considered important for their own well-being, as well as that of their community, state, and nation. Often these included broad-reaching concerns that were the precursors of those that led to the wider social reform that overlapped this time period. These annual presentations provide a richer and deeper insight into the goals, developing philosophy, and changing ideals of the WSHS and are an indication of what was happening on a larger scale within the state.

However, the published proceedings obviously reflect the ideas and beliefs of a group that was overwhelmingly Anglo-American, fairly well-educated, and English-speaking, at least during the society's early years, and targeted a readership with similar ethnic and social backgrounds. There is little evidence of much attention to, or interest in, the equally strong garden traditions and history of the much larger groups of non-English European immigrants who were settling in Wisconsin during this same period.[3] Despite this limitation, the amateur and professional horticulturists who composed the WSHS provided, through the society's written records, a fascinating and previously unstudied view of the aspirations and ideals of a specific cultural group united in its belief that horticultural knowledge and practice led to an improved lifestyle. Scattered throughout the settled areas of Wisconsin, these farmers, businessmen, club women, academic faculty, and nurserymen enthusiastically supported and initiated agricultural and horticultural changes throughout the state. As older members died and a younger group of emerging academics and professionals entered the arena, the publications

PETUNIA

recorded nostalgic recollections intermixed with excitement about emerging ideas. Discussions about farm improvement, women's suffrage, village improvement, or war gardens mirrored the social, economic, and political concerns of the state during this era.

The WSHS occasionally published recommended reading lists on various gardening or farming topics for its members. In the course of unearthing this sometimes obscure primary literature, I discovered that one nationally known nineteenth-century author, Eben Rexford, wrote six popular gardening books from his home in Shiocton, just west of Green Bay, while several others, including Liberty Hyde Bailey, O. C. Simonds, and Frank J. Scott, had strong regional ties to the Midwest. My initial belief that all the nineteenth-century garden writing originated along the eastern seaboard was therefore incorrect: the books and magazines may have been published in New York, Boston, or Philadelphia, but their authors were just as likely to be from Michigan or Wisconsin or Ohio. This suggests a possible correlation between national and regional garden styles. Additionally, around the turn of the twentieth century, the uniquely Midwestern "Prairie style" of landscape architecture developed by Wilhelm Miller, O. C. Simonds, Jens Jensen, and others was gaining recognition at the national level, thereby encouraging a regional approach to garden design. WSHS speakers often included references to both national and regional writers; clearly a state horticultural society was a useful conduit for the distribution and dissemination of national horticultural ideals.

Photographs of gardens and homes were important sources during my research. Although the first photographs did not appear in WSHS publications until the late 1800s, earlier collections on file at the Wisconsin Historical Society include images of gardens and homes around the state. The Andreas Larsen Dahl and Charles Van Schaick photographic collections are particularly useful records of Wisconsin landscapes during the 1870–1900 period. As cameras became more universally available during the first decades of the twentieth century, photographs of Wisconsin gardens and homes were increasingly included in WSHS publications, often as examples of the ideal.

The recommended plant lists discussed in chapter 5 and listed in the appendix are simply a consolidated record of what the WSHS was advising for success in the Wisconsin garden, rather than a comprehensive inventory of all that was available at the time. For more information about the dates of introduction and varieties of specific plants and seeds, please refer to the books listed in the selected bibliography. These are important resources for the historical gardener, and their existence underscores an increasing national interest not only in gardening for its own sake but also in unearthing vernacular garden history. Numerous online sites also provide almost limitless, though not necessarily accurate, information on the same topic. Most important, several Wisconsin historic sites are either establishing or have already established accurate period gardens that illustrate different aspects of Wisconsin settlement and garden history. Each is unique, and all well worth a visit.

SWEET PEA

As I worked my way through the literature, photographs, and archival material, I sometimes felt as though I were exploring one of those dense, dark shrubberies that were so popular with the English aristocracy in previous centuries: winding pathways that led to blind alleys and impenetrable thickets; interesting unidentifiable overhanging branches and undergrowth; rough walkways; and too many intriguing corners inviting more exploration. I found such a treasure trove of material that I could have easily spent the next ten years processing it all.

This book is simply the beginning. It identifies various little-known but easily accessible resources that clarify questions about the appearance and composition of the Wisconsin vernacular garden during the mid- to late nineteenth and early twentieth centuries. It also provides a foundation for further research into individual home gardens, whether public or private. I have included guidelines and recommendations for that complex but worthwhile undertaking in chapter 6.

I hope that *Vintage Wisconsin Gardens* will encourage you to delve more deeply into the intriguing and fascinating history of the Wisconsin cultural landscape and its early gardens, and also offer guidance for incorporating some of these ideas into your own vintage garden.

Changing Ideals in Nineteenth-Century American Vernacular Gardens

And how much happiness, how much pure pleasure, that strengthens and invigorates our best and holiest affections, is there not experienced in bestowing upon our homes something of grace and loveliness—in making the place dearest to our hearts a sunny spot where the social sympathies take shelter securely under the shadowy eaves, or grow and entwine trustfully with the tall trees or wreathed vines that cluster around, as if striving to shut out whatever of bitterness or strife may be found in the open highways of the world.

ANDREW JACKSON DOWNING, 1842[1]

merican garden historians have noted that the layout and appearance of eighteenth- and nineteenth-century eastern seaboard vernacular gardens strongly resembled the English "cottage garden" of the time period, although the English vernacular garden had itself undergone centuries of modification.[2]

In the United States, its typical form by the early 1800s was a small, enclosed dooryard immediately in front of the house. It contained a mixture of shrubs, flowers, vines, herbs, and vegetables, "for meate and medicine, for use and for delight," and its maintenance was generally the responsibility of the woman of the house.[3] Fruit bushes and orchard trees were located either to the side or the rear of the house. Some varieties of herbs and vegetables had been introduced to settlers by local Indians, who also taught the newcomers their techniques of planting crops such as corn, squash, and beans

This North Yorkshire garden depicted by Sue Firth illustrates the English "cottage garden" elements incorporated in eighteenth-century eastern seaboard dooryard gardens. Framing the front door, these enclosed gardens usually contained a mix of annual and perennial flowers, vines, herbs, vegetables, and small shrubs.

KILBURN, NORTH YORKSHIRE, ENGLAND FROM AN ORIGINAL PAINTING BY SUE FIRTH FROM THE GATEHOUSE COLLECTION, WWW.GATEHOUSEPRINTS.COM

in more efficient hills rather than rows.[4] These would be planted in a separate area behind the house.

The rising interest in American horticulture in the late eighteenth century had been spearheaded in large part by George Washington and Thomas Jefferson, both of whom were passionate amateur horticulturists with the means to design and build substantial estates. Landscape historian Diane Kostial McGuire has noted that their gardens (at Mount Vernon and Monticello, respectively) can be described as the first specifically American designed landscapes, although both show marked adherence to the Italian and English landscape styles, with large open vistas, juxtaposition of formality and informality, the use of trees and shrubs rather than masses of color, and the inclusion of exotic species.[5] While Washington and Jefferson were highly esteemed national leaders, their horticultural influence was probably more visible on large estates than in smaller vernacular gardens. A more important legacy for American gardeners may have come from Jefferson's resolve that the Lewis and Clark expedition of 1804–1806 collect botanical specimens during their exploration of the interior of America. Seeds and plants from that journey were classified, propagated, and made available to the public during the ensuing years by Philadelphia nurserymen Bernard M'Mahon and William Hamilton, thus expanding the vegetative varieties grown in vernacular gardens.[6]

Andrew Jackson Downing was the first landscape gardener to bring the concept of rural home landscaping to the American public. In his 1841 *A Treatise on the Theory and Practice of Landscape Gardening Adapted to North America*, Downing included plans for rural homes as well as their gardens, often showing the idealized rural home as a small, Gothic Revival–inspired cottage with a carefully planted landscape that included native trees and shrubs and imparted an overall feeling of neatness and order.

By including specific plans for homes as well as their grounds, Downing was suggesting the importance of the cohesion of building style and its surrounding landscape. Downing wrote extensively on garden design in *The Horticulturist*, which he edited until his death in 1852. The magazine, published between 1846 and 1875, was the best-known and most popular garden journal of its time.

Downing was a colleague of Calvert Vaux and Frederick Law Olmsted and an early supporter of what would later become New York's Central Park, which was designed by Olmsted and Vaux. Olmsted's distinguished career spanned the latter half of the nineteenth century, and his legacy can be seen to this day in public parks, cemeteries, and residential estates. In 1869 Olmsted and Vaux designed Riverside, the first suburban community in America, just outside Chicago, on the banks of the Des Plaines River.

Andrew Jackson Downing's 1842 design for "A Cottage in the English or Rural Gothic Style" emphasized steep and irregular rooflines. The landscape framed the home, which stood in a somewhat elevated position.
COTTAGE RESIDENCES, 1847

Fig. 9.

Note the open front lawn and framework of trees and shrubbery in Jacob Weidenmann's 1870 plan for a suburban home and landscape.

BEAUTIFYING COUNTRY HOMES, 1870

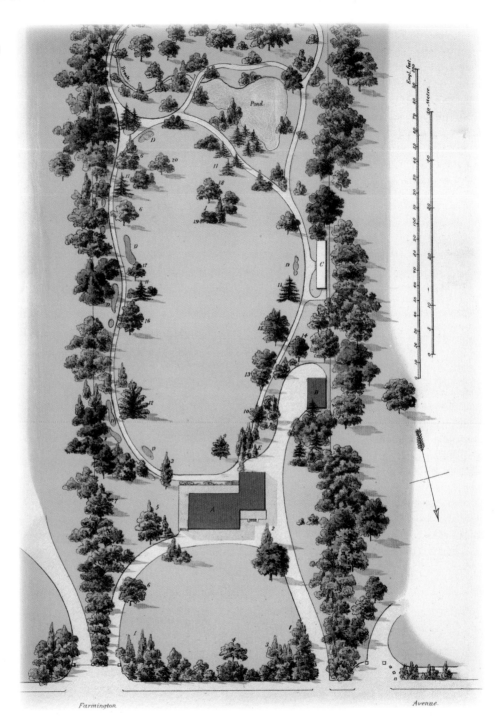

Weidenmann and others espoused interconnected front lawns on suburban streets. His plan included unbroken areas of front lawn, attractive entrances, and small shrubs that mirrored the horizontal line of the street.

BEAUTIFYING COUNTRY HOMES, 1870

The village, now a National Historic Landmark, has curvilinear streets that conform to the natural rolling topography, homes set back on deep lots, heavily planted spacious parks and open areas for recreation, and a rural feel.[7] Olmsted was probably most familiar to Wisconsin residents as the site designer for Milwaukee's Lake and Washington parks as well as the enormously popular and well-attended 1893 World's Columbian Exposition in Chicago. The formally landscaped grounds that surrounded the magnificent Beaux Arts buildings of the "White City" and the naturalistic planting design of Wooded Isle were planned and executed by Olmsted.

Olmsted's many disciples included the architect and engineer Jacob Weidenmann, who later became his partner. Weidenmann's 1870 *Beautifying Country Homes* is lavishly illustrated with hand-colored plates of landscape plans for suburban home grounds of varying size and shape. The plans show curvilinear driveways, neatly outlined walkways, and large expanses of lawn at the front and sides of the dwelling, with clothes yards, vegetable gardens, and barns to the rear, thus suggesting differentiation between public and private space.[8] Weidenmann also suggested that neighboring front yards on suburban streets should be linked by complementary landscape design treatments rather than divided by street or side front-yard fences.

Weidenmann's book was one of many that illustrated plans for intricate cutout beds in the front lawn, a fashion that had reemerged in England during the mid-nineteenth

Patterns for carpet beds were regularly included in most garden books of the 1870s to 1890s. The directions for creating and planting them could sometimes be quite complex.

HOME FLORICULTURE, 1890

This vibrant circular carpet bed in front of the Cotton House at Heritage Hill State Historical Park in Green Bay contains a variety of brightly colored heirloom annuals including marigolds, celosia, coleus, and petunias.

JIM DOCKENDORFF

Bottom left: An example of the very popular late-nineteenth-century tropical bed, which could contain canna lilies, *Amaranthus caudatus*, caladium, coleus, and feverfew.

VICK'S MONTHLY MAGAZINE, APRIL 1880

Bottom right: Modern example of a tropical bed at Villa Louis in Prairie du Chien

LEE SOMERVILLE

century after the increased availability of glass for conservatories made mass production of annual plants possible. Based on the parterre beds of Versailles and other large French estates, "carpet beds" in the shape of squares, diamonds, hexagons, and other patterns contained mass plantings of annual flowers, tender exotics, and low-growing shrubs that formed a colorful geometric design suggestive of the patterns seen in Oriental rugs.[9] Circular or star-shaped "tropical" beds composed of massed tall annuals such as canna lilies and castor bean plants were also popular choices for the front lawn.

Beautifying Country Homes was published in the same year as Frank J. Scott's *The Art of Beautifying Suburban Home Grounds of Small Extent*, which contained similar plans for suburban homes and their grounds. Scott, an architect, landscape designer, and real estate developer who had previous connections to both Downing and Vaux, has been credited with introducing the American concept of the "front lawn" as decorative space in his suburban designs for his hometown of Toledo, Ohio.[10] His popular book included twenty-four plates with plans for suburban home and grounds layouts.[11]

Scott detailed the steps needed to create complicated topiary structures, especially for the entrances to his gardens. He cautioned that these living sculptures could take up to ten years to mature into their final form.

Horace William Shaler Cleveland, who had relocated from Massachusetts to Chicago in 1869, was another well-known landscape designer. In 1873 he published *Landscape Architecture, As Applied to the Wants of the West*, a regionally specific work in the emerging field of landscape architecture in which he used the term *landscape architecture* despite his misgivings:

> [T]he term "landscape architecture" is objectionable, as being only figuratively expressive of the art it is used to designate. I make use of it, under protest, as the readiest means of making myself understood, in the absence of a more appropriate term.[12]

Cleveland's 1873 definition of the term was as follows: "Landscape gardening, or more properly, Landscape Architecture is the art of arranging land so as to adapt it most conveniently, economically and gracefully, to any of the varied wants of civilization."[13]

Cleveland's major objective in his book was to outline his planning philosophy for communities that were developing in the American West as a result of railroad advancement across the country. He despised the rectangular grid system whereby towns were platted with no relationship to the underlying topography and natural features. Using examples he saw along the Mississippi and Missouri rivers, he argued that the founders had "bequeathed to all future generations of inhabitants, a legacy of

Left: This 1870 garden plan illustrates the use of carpet beds around the edge of the front lawn and is an early example of suburban lot size and layout.

THE ART OF BEAUTIFYING SUBURBAN HOME GROUNDS OF SMALL EXTENT, 1870

Right: Frank J. Scott and others encouraged the use of topiary.

THE ART OF BEAUTIFYING SUBURBAN HOME GROUNDS OF SMALL EXTENT, 1870

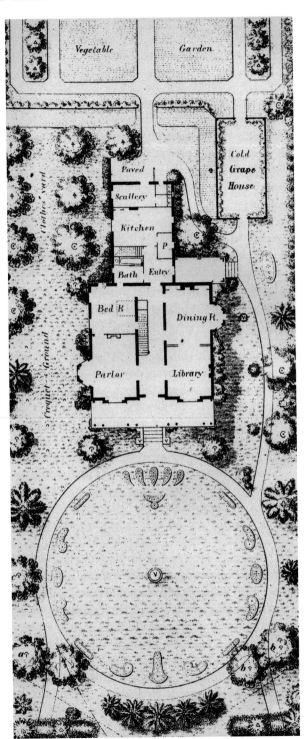

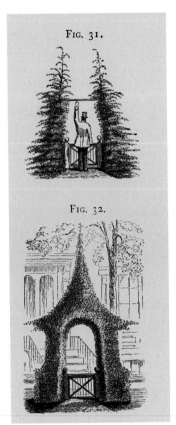

taxation, to preserve the hideousness of the original outrage on common sense and subdivisions to the natural shape of the ground," and he reiterated the importance of retaining the natural features and topography unique to a place.[14]

On a smaller scale, Cleveland discussed in detail the landscape designs of rural estates, including the methods he used to select the location of the home and outbuildings to take advantage of local topography and the separation of public and private spaces.[15] Cleveland continued to work in the Midwest, moving in 1886 from Chicago to Minneapolis, where he developed the Twin Cities' metropolitan parks system, described by one author as "his major professional triumph and perhaps America's finest urban open space network."[16]

Cleveland was unimpressed with the quality of the increasing number of "books and treatises upon landscape gardening and rural art" that appeared with the burgeoning interest in home gardening in the aftermath of the post–Civil War economic depression.[17] Many of these bore titles that included the words *home grounds*, but Cleveland felt that many of their authors concerned themselves only with decorative aspects of the landscape and did not address the basic underlying need for careful site planning.[18]

The Olmsted office produced an equally significant landscape architect: Warren H. Manning, who in 1899 became a founding member of the American Society of Landscape Architects and who was an articulate spokesman for the emerging profession. His work included campus and park designs in several states, including Wisconsin, where, among other projects, he designed the landscape for the Stout Manual Training School in Menomonie in 1899. Shortly after completing this project, he published *A Handbook for Planning and Planting Small Home Grounds*, which contained "a list of native and commonly cultivated plants that are represented in the collection upon the Stout Manual Training School Grounds."[19] This text was recommended to members of the Wisconsin State Horticultural Society by its secretary Frederic Cranefield and formed the basis of the society's prescriptive literature for home grounds after 1900. With its promotion of the use of native plants, foundation plantings, and a more organic and naturalistic appearance of the grounds of public areas, Manning's text provided a foretaste of the changing ideals in landscape gardening around the turn of the twentieth century.[20]

During the same period, two notable Chicago landscape gardeners (their preferred title) were independently developing a unique Midwestern naturalistic style of landscape design that became known as the "prairie spirit in landscape gardening."[21] O. C. Simonds, in his employment as landscape gardener at Graceland Cemetery, and Jens Jensen, the superintendent of Chicago's West Park Commission, brought into their designs such elements as native vegetation, natural features such as local stone, and the gentle flowing organic lines they observed in the prairies and woodlands outside the city. They organized the Chicago Parks Commission and were influential members of the Prairie Club, the Cliff Dwellers, and Friends of Our Native Landscape, organizations that celebrated and attempted to preserve aspects of the distinctive Midwestern landscapes. Simonds later expressed his philosophy of landscape gardening as being a combination of unity, harmony, and balance.[22]

❧ GARDENING IDEAS ❧

These late-nineteenth- and early-twentieth-century magazines and journals were mined by Wisconsin gardeners in search of inspiration.

TITLE	DATES OF PUBLICATION	PLACE OF PUBLICATION
The Horticulturist	1846–1875	Albany, New York
Harper's Bazaar	1850–present	New York
The Delineator	1873–1937	New York
The Gardener's Monthly and Horticulturist	1876–1888	Philadelphia
Ladies' Home Journal	1883–present	Philadelphia
Good Housekeeping	1885–present	New York
Garden and Forest	1888–1897	New York
Woman's Home Companion	1896–1957	Springfield, Ohio
House Beautiful	1896–present	New York
McCall's	1897–2001	New York
The Craftsman	1901–1916	New York
Keith's Magazine	1901–1930	Minneapolis
House & Garden	1901–2007	New York
American Homes and Gardens	1905–1915	New York
The Garden Magazine	1905–1924	New York
Country Life in America	1907–1917	New York
Better Homes and Gardens	1924–present	Des Moines
American Home	1928–1978	New York

The development of the discipline and profession of landscape architecture, as distinct from landscape gardening, gathered momentum in 1899 when the American Society of Landscape Architects was formed; the following year the landscape architecture program at Harvard University was established. However, the terms *landscape architecture* and *landscape gardening* were sometimes used interchangeably. The Department of Horticulture at the University of Wisconsin offered courses in landscape gardening as early as 1904, hiring Franz Aust to direct the program in 1915. A specific degree in landscape architecture was offered within the Department of Horticulture in 1926. William Longnecker joined the faculty in 1929, and the program continued as part of the Horticulture Department until 1964, when it was reorganized into the Department of Landscape Architecture.[23]

Despite the growing importance of landscape architecture as a profession, most home gardeners relied on magazines and books for ideas on garden making. Gardening and shelter (home) magazines with garden pages were an increasingly available option even on the frontier, although most were published in the eastern states.

One of the most frequently recommended garden books during the mid-nineteenth century was Massachusetts seedsman Joseph Breck's *The Flower-Garden; Or, Breck's Book of Flowers; in Which are Described All the Various Hardy Herbaceous Perennials, Annuals, Shrubby Plants, and Evergreen Trees, Desirable for Ornamental Purposes, With Directions for their Cultivation*, published in 1851.[24] The major portion of this work is a list of suitable flowers for the small garden; however, in the first brief chapter, Breck suggested ideas for its layout, including the use of square, rectangular, or more "fanciful" shaped beds surrounded by wide gravel walks, much like miniature versions of French parterre gardens and a forerunner of the carpet beds described by Weidenmann and others. The following excerpt epitomizes the contemporary garden ideal that the garden should form a neat picture, either framed in a window or by its boundaries:

> *Neatness should be the prevailing characteristic of a flower-garden, which should be so situated as to form an ornamental appendage to the house; and when circumstances will admit, placed before windows exposed to a southern or south-eastern aspect. The principle on which it should be laid out ought to be that of exhibiting a variety of colors and forms, so blended as to produce one beautiful whole. In a small flower-garden, viewed from the windows of the house, this effect is best produced by beds or borders, formed on the side of each other, and parallel to the windows from whence they are seen.*[25]

Similar declarations were seen frequently in both national and regional garden literature.

Spring Time in the Country appeared in *Harper's Weekly* in 1868. This illustration clearly promotes the ideal that working together in the garden was a healthy family activity.

COURTESY OF STRONG NATIONAL MUSEUM OF PLAY, ROCHESTER, NY

As the lawn mower became more available in America in the 1860s, larger swaths of grass could be more easily maintained, thereby creating an outdoor "parlor" for family recreation.[26] At the same time, in the wake of the economic and cultural unrest that followed the Civil War, outdoor activities like croquet and even light gardening became not only popular but highly recommended for the maintenance of a healthy lifestyle, especially for women and children. The resulting move into the garden transformed it from merely pictorial to usable space.

By the late 1880s, some fashionable English and American gardens included elements that echoed the highly decorative and often elaborate interior furnishings of the period. Ornamental trellises, statuary, garden urns, furniture, topiary, and weeping varieties of small ornamental trees reflected the style of ornate furniture and patterned textiles of the front parlor.[27]

In America, the Colonial nostalgia that followed the 1876 Centennial Exposition in Philadelphia had resulted in the appearance, in the 1880s, of Colonial Revival furniture, architecture, and even gardens, especially along America's eastern seaboard.

Garden elements included formal entryways, parterres, and symmetrical plantings that accented the house style and were reminiscent of classical European estate plantings.

This Colonial nostalgia was sometimes interpreted quite differently, especially in vernacular gardens. Labeled the "old-fashioned," "nostalgic," or "grandmother's" gardens, they featured flowers that had supposedly been popular in the early 1800s, especially perennials such as roses, phlox, hollyhocks, honeysuckle, daylilies, verbena, and lilacs. These were massed in curving borders and allowed to flow around and into the pathways, in the style of the original dooryards. Colonial historian Alice Morse Earle was the best-known proponent of this type of garden, which was popularized in her 1901 *Old Time Gardens.*

At the same time in England, artist and gardener Gertrude Jekyll had already begun to design herbaceous borders with drifts of color and a naturalistic feel, in a style that suited proponents of the Arts & Crafts movement. Jekyll's approach to gardening was to treat it like fine art:

> *In practice, it is to place every plant or group of plants with such thoughtful care and definite intention that they shall form part of a harmonious whole, and the successive portions or in some cases even single details, shall show a series of pictures.*[28]

Jekyll had an enormous influence on garden design throughout the first half of the twentieth century in England and, to a lesser extent, in America. The nostalgic garden remained fashionable during the first decades of the twentieth century and included a revival of interest in using native plants in the home landscape.[29]

At the same time, the divergence of landscape architecture and landscape gardening continued. While the wealthy relied on landscape architects to design their large estates, ordinary homeowners took advantage of the plethora of available gardening resources to plant and maintain their gardens. Popular books included those of Liberty Hyde Bailey, a landscape gardener whose work was frequently recommended to Wisconsin State Horticultural Society members. As a professor of horticulture at Michigan State Agricultural College, Bailey had organized the Department of Horticulture and Landscape Gardening in 1885. In 1888 he created a similar program at Cornell University in Ithaca, New York. In addition to the massive *Cyclopaedia of American Horticulture,* published in four volumes between 1900 and 1902, Bailey wrote numerous garden books in a readable style that were reprinted time and again. His casual approach to gardening and plants must have been particularly refreshing and enjoyable for the inexperienced gardener. For example, in *Manual of Gardening,* a compendium of his earlier works, he stated that:

Exuberant flowers spill over onto each other in this 1913 example of a nostalgic or grandmother's garden in Ripon. This garden style was popularized by Alice Morse Earle in the early 1900s.

WISCONSIN HORTICULTURE, MARCH 1913

A modern example of a nostalgic garden at Heritage Flower Farm in Mukwonago

BETTY ADELMAN

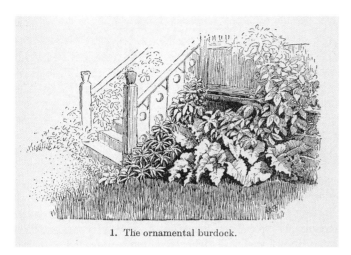

1. The ornamental burdock.

[A] patch of lusty pigweeds, growing and crowding in luxuriant abandon may be a better and more worthy object of affection than a bed of coleus in which every spark of life and spirit and individuality has been sheared out and suppressed. The man who worries day and night about the dandelions in the lawn will find great relief in loving the dandelions.[30]

He also illustrated the use of common burdock as a foundation planting for a difficult corner of the yard.[31]

Changing ideals: Liberty Hyde Bailey saw no reason not to make use of every corner and every plant—including burdock.

GARDEN-MAKING, 1898

Bailey's well-illustrated works contained a wealth of information for the ordinary gardener. He was editor of *American Garden* (1890–1893) and *Country Life in America* (1907–1917).[32] His influence is strongly apparent in various publications of the WSHS, and several of his books were recommended in the reading lists occasionally included in *Wisconsin Horticulture*.

Another popular author often recommended to Wisconsin readers was Eben Rexford, the author of *Vick's Home Floriculture*, published in 1890. James Vick was a well-known seedsman who, by 1886, had established a five-story mail-order seed store in Rochester, New York. As part of his enterprise, he also published the nationally distributed *Vick's Monthly Magazine* that included gardening advice and columns, short stories, and sentimental poetry of general interest as well as lavish illustrations. Rexford, a frequent contributor to the magazine since its inaugural issue in 1886, was chosen by Vick to write *Vick's Home Floriculture* because of his extensive knowledge of plants, reader recognition, and "easy and familiar style."[33] The book became a national best seller and today provides important documentation of American garden history.[34] It included advice on garden design and the layout of beds, care of indoor and outdoor plants, and a list of commonly used annuals and perennials. Rexford also presented designs for cutout beds for carpet bedding and instructions for a tropical bed consisting of castor bean plants, canna lilies, caladiums, and coleus.

Rexford was a prolific short-story writer, poet, and lyricist, as well as an expert self-taught horticulturist. Between 1890 and 1915, the year of his death, he not only published six additional gardening books but also was the garden editor for the popular national magazine *Ladies' Home Journal* for five years. He managed his busy career from his home in Shiocton, a tiny village just west of Green Bay, and reportedly left Wisconsin only on one occasion: to

meet with his publishers and attend the 1876 Centennial Exposition in Philadelphia.[35] His later books included photographs of gardens, presumably images he'd taken in and around his hometown in northeastern Wisconsin. Rexford was a strong advocate for the use of vines, especially Virginia creeper (known at the time as *Ampelopsis* but later reclassified as *Parthenocissus quinquefolia*). He also advocated the use of curved borders heavily planted with mixed perennials to provide texture, height, color, and seasonal interest.[36]

Like Alice Morse Earle and Grace Tabor in the United States, and Gertrude Jekyll in England, Rexford favored simple, natural-looking gardens with appropriately rustic decorative elements. This passage from *Vick's Home Floriculture*, in which he criticizes an apparently common garden embellishment, is often cited by landscape historians:

> *I do really hope that no reader of this book ever had the "Gypsy Kettle" craze. If he or she has, I trust that they have recovered from it long ago. The sight of a dinner pot, painted a fiery red, and dangling from three sticks with a poor down-hearted little plant in it has often made me feel like committing trespass.*[37]

Rexford's 1916 *The Making of a Home* combined his plans for building a country house and garden with a somewhat sentimental but fairly typical vision of the simple and rewarding family life that would result from physical labor. The photographs Rexford used to illustrate his book—many of them Wisconsin subjects—and others have significance beyond the focus of this book. They provide invaluable, little-known documentation of early-twentieth-century vernacular home landscapes.

Although not landscape architects, Bailey and Rexford did not hesitate to provide detailed instructions on the layout of home grounds, including advice on home placement on the lot, drainage, soil composition, and plant placement, as well as detailed lists of plant varieties and general gardening advice. Their careers spanned the turn of the twentieth century, and their books were reprinted well into the 1930s, maintaining relevance as gardens were modified to reflect social changes.

Economic hardship, political corruption, and a rising concern for the social welfare of the working class, women, and children combined to produce significant changes in the social culture of the state and the country at the turn of the twentieth century. Wisconsin's politicians led the way in the resulting period of reform known as the Progressive Era.

❦ THE EVOLUTION OF A GARDEN ❦

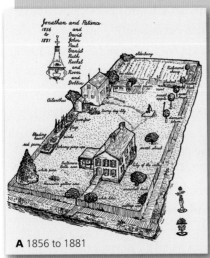

A 1856 to 1881

B 1881 to 1906

C 1906 to 1931

In "The Stylish House," Illinois ecologist, naturalist, artist, and writer May Theilgaard Watts (1893–1975) neatly summarized the evolution of garden style and taste from 1856 to 1963. This essay, which appeared in her *Reading the Landscape of America*, included a series of sketches, five of which are reproduced here.

This imagined small-town Midwestern home, based on Watts's research of primary literature, is shown as it underwent several generations of ownership and successive changes in garden fashion.[1] As was typical in the middle years of the nineteenth century, the garden in the first sketch (**A**) was planted with a few native trees and shrubs, including lilac bushes on either side of the front gate, rose bushes along the fence, and the popular flowers of the time period—peonies, hollyhocks, iris, and

Johnny-jump-ups—planted in a straight bed along the side fence. The large vegetable garden at the rear of the lot has room for several small fruit bushes and trees. The second owners followed fashion by creating circular and star-shaped carpet beds in the lawn, and adding a fountain, statuary, and a decorative fence (**B**). But by the turn of the twentieth century, a new style of gardening had emerged and carpet beds and bright colors were no longer considered in vogue. The third owners of Watts's imagined home followed the then current recommendations and eliminated the circular beds, replaced the fence with a shrub boundary, extended and curved the perennial bed, planted a row of Lombardy poplars, and installed a rock garden for succulents such as hens and chicks and other newly available Mediterranean plants (**C**).

❧ THE EVOLUTION OF A GARDEN ❧

D 1941 to 1963

E 1963

ILLUSTRATIONS FROM *READING THE LANDSCAPE OF AMERICA*, BY MAY THEILGAARD WATTS, © 1975, 2003 BY ESTATE OF MAY THEILGAARD WATTS; USED BY PERMISSION OF NATURE STUDY GUILD PUBLISHERS

Note the subdivision of the lot and subsequent decrease in the size of the vegetable garden, the conversion of the old barn into a garage with a wide driveway, heavy foundation planting, and an open lawn.

The post–World War II period brought more change to the garden (**D**). Picket fences and bare foundation walls once again found favor, as did vegetable or "victory" gardens. Individual shrubs accented the corners of the house, while the rectangular rose beds added another geometric element to the yard.

By 1963, the original house is all that is recognizable on the lot (**E**). Road widening projects, a further subdivision of the lot, and a large paved driveway had left the old house isolated in a sea of concrete. The garden consists of a large berm, several huge boulders, and a few low-maintenance shrubs.

These illustrations exemplify the definition of the vernacular garden: that it is the product of the interrelationship between the owners of the house and their garden, that it contains several incompletely erased layers, and that it does change fairly dramatically over time. Through her examples of a home garden that was subject to changing fashions, Watts was depicting "fashion as an ecological factor."[2]

NOTES

1. May Theilgaard Watts, "The Stylish House," in *Reading the Landscape of America* (New York: Collier Books, 1975), 320–345. Watts used a number of garden and style books of the period to develop the essay and drawings of this imagined home.

2. Ibid., 324.

Changes in the laws that governed the rights of workers, women, and children and eventually led to women's suffrage (ratified in Wisconsin in 1919) also indirectly changed the landscape. Local civic enhancement organizations, often led by women, encouraged community involvement in municipal concerns such as the disposal of sewage and waste, efficient transportation systems, and the improvement of school services. The organizations also advocated for the improvement of community landscapes such as school grounds, street plantings and lighting, and local parks.

The American Civic Association, founded in 1907, spearheaded the movement. One of its board members was writer Zona Gale, who lived in Portage. In 1913 she wrote "Civic Improvement in the Little Towns," a pamphlet based on her work in her hometown. In it, Gale discussed how to coordinate local organizations including women's clubs to address civic issues and even the design of home gardens with a more democratic base than had been common in the late nineteenth century. Gale wrote:

> *The new spirit of community realization is to the old idea of "improving" what the new principle of constructive philanthropy is to the proceedings of the Lord and Lady Bountiful of mere charity. The new way of civic work is the way, not of paternalism, but of humanhood.*[38]

The improved economy led to better employment opportunities, especially in the manufacturing trades, which attracted young men away from farm life and household servants into better-paying factory jobs. Meanwhile, in Wisconsin, as in other parts of the country, increased crime, dirt, and noise pushed wealthier city dwellers to relocate to the developing suburbs, where they relied on improved transportation networks for easy access to the city. They wanted smaller, more efficient homes that were easier to maintain than large, many-roomed Victorian houses. The new ideal was the Craftsman house, introduced in 1903 by then New Yorker Gustav Stickley, who had been influenced by the English Arts & Crafts movement that fifty years earlier had developed as a reaction to increased mechanization and industrialization. Through his magazine *The Craftsman*, Stickley promoted a return to a simpler lifestyle, in which creativity and individual craftsmanship once again became an important element in architectural and furnishing style.[39]

The Craftsman house, plans for which were easily available through *The Craftsman*, included more open space with easier traffic flow; an informal living room that replaced the formal Victorian parlor; larger and brighter kitchens; and the inclusion of front, side, and back porches. These design changes eventually led to a corresponding change in garden design, expressed as a more organic interconnection between interior and exterior living spaces united

As architecture changed, homes and gardens became more unified. In this example, the bungalow's porches, the vines, and foundation plantings are interconnected.
THE LANDSCAPE GARDENING BOOK, 1911

by porches, terraces, or verandas and the use of natural building materials.[40] According to garden historian Patricia Tice, other visible signs of the changing function and appearance of the garden were foundation plantings around the base of the house, easier access to the garden, and private garden rooms. As a result, boundaries and edges—both between the house and its garden and between adjoining lots—were softened and blurred with vegetation.

By the 1920s increasing numbers of landscape architects began to address the design needs of the small vernacular garden. Representative of these was Fletcher Steele, an early graduate of the Harvard program and a former assistant to Warren H. Manning. In 1924 he wrote *Design in the Little Garden*, which his editor justified the need for with a sharp critique of the average Midwestern town:

> *Many of us with little ground are, as yet, entirely ignorant of the special need for design, for plan in little spaces. And this fact, and the lack of any town-plan, are the foremost reasons for the absolute ugliness of the average small town of say the Middle West.*[41]

Steele himself had a more relaxed approach, stating that even the familiar could appear beautiful.[42] His approach in this relevant work was very similar to that of Gertrude Jekyll and Grace Tabor in the use of curved borders, soft colors, and focal points of statuary or natural features. Steele designed outdoor rooms, sometimes paved and canopied, with open sides that permitted the gradual passage from inside to outside.

His "green garden" was an enclosed area of lawn, either grass or ground cover, and few flowers, which served as a peaceful outdoor room close to the house.[43]

Like Jekyll and others, Steele was careful in his use of color, requiring that flowers complemented green foliage. Reds and magentas had lost popularity in the garden, and Steele concurred that "magenta flowers are almost never in harmonious relation to the green foliage of their own plants."[44] Both Tabor and Steele abhorred the Victorian fashion of carpet bedding, and in 1911 Tabor commented:

> *The flower bed habit . . . surely this is the greatest abomination of all! It is going to die hard, even with those who truly wish to kill it. Many there are, alas! who will not wish to; for its star, and its crescent, its circle and its triangle have so impressed themselves upon its victims, that they cannot see a stretch of smooth and velvet turf without an instant temptation to throw themselves on it and carve some of those mystic symbols from its heart.*[45]

Steele was no less critical:

> *Of such were flower beds during the sixties and seventies of the last century when stars, circles and crescents were stuffed with conspicuous plants in ugly, grotesque combinations. Huge caladiums and canna leaves burst from wretched lines of coleus, ice plant and houseleeks.*[46]

These two statements underline the change in prevailing garden fashion. The social reform that affected all aspects of home life during the late nineteenth and early twentieth centuries also led to a change in the appearance of the vernacular garden. The Victorian-era formal beds filled with colorful annual bedding plants fell out of fashion and were replaced with softer, more graceful perennials in more muted colors planted in borders surrounding the lawns and driveways. Enclosed front gardens were opened up, while private, enclosed areas for work and recreation grew larger. The concept of a softer, more organic interrelationship between house and garden was exaggerated by the use of foundation plantings; the use of natural materials on porches, trellises, and pathways; and a looser trimming of trees and shrubs rather than the geometric topiary shapes favored in the late 1800s.

Wisconsin gardeners certainly had access to the national ideas about gardens and garden making. How they adapted and translated these ideas to fit their own particular landscape is a story in itself—a story that adds another intriguing and unfamiliar chapter to Wisconsin's settlement history.

From Farmstead to Village

Even in my recollection, surrounding groves and pastures were gorgeous with beauties now preserved only in a few rare gardens or by an occasional enterprising florist, and I recently paid several dollars for a volume, containing pictures of flowers which I gathered by the apronful when a child. Hardy golden rods and wild asters seem to follow settlement, and replace the tenderer painted cup, wild phlox, butterfly flower, gentian, forget-me not, moccasin flower, and others.

MRS. IDA TILSON, 1891[1]

he struggles that immigrants underwent as they strove to establish their farmsteads and communities were underscored by the unforgiving and unfamiliar terrain and climate of their newly adopted home. The stark and isolated landscape of the Northwest Territory undoubtedly contrasted strikingly with their previous homelands, whether a populated eastern seaboard Yankee town or a rural northern European village.

By the early 1800s this landscape had undergone several modifications, both physical and cultural. These changes explain the pattern of settlement that developed during the early nineteenth century and are therefore key to understanding how gardens developed and changed over the course of the century and beyond.

The physical characteristics of the region are defined by the effects of glaciation that encompassed most of the present boundaries of the state and left glacial and

meltwater landforms such as eskers, moraines, and outwash plains. The Driftless Area in the southwestern portion of the state, with its rolling topography and deep river valleys, is equally defined by the absence of these effects.[2] The northern upland white pine forests and the mixed deciduous and coniferous forests in the middle tier of the state contrasted with the prairie soils, oak openings, and meadows of the southern section.

The rivers and streams interwoven throughout the region had provided transportation routes for generations of indigenous people who utilized the nutrient-rich topsoils formed by sedimentation for agricultural purposes. The mining of rich deposits of iron ore and lead in the northern and southwestern portions of the region, respectively, had begun long before Europeans entered the area. Food was plentiful, much of it hunted, fished, and gathered from the thick forests, fertile prairie meadows, lakeshores, and rivers. For thousands of years before white settlement, Indians had relied on the land for shelter, food, and medicine. But in the space of two hundred years following the first European contact in 1648, indigenous people were dislodged from the land they had lived on for generations, pushed westward by land-hungry Europeans who, after exhausting the fur trade market, now demanded and obtained settlement rights.[3]

French explorers had led the way for fur trading operations that encompassed the area between the bay of Green Bay along the Fox and Wisconsin rivers and extended to the Mississippi River during the seventeenth and eighteenth centuries. Small settlements along the waterways were laid out using the French long-lot system that ensured waterfront access to each title holder. Fish, game, wild berries, and seeds supplemented by Indian crops that included corn and squash provided a reasonable diet for these early pioneers.

The escalating desire for beaver skins, used for hats in fashionable European cities, led to intense trading with the Indians. The Louisiana Purchase of 1803 and the Treaty of Ghent in 1812 ensured expanded American ownership of the continent, and as the results of the Lewis and Clark expedition became public, exploration and settlement of the West increased.

The next layer of the palimpsest was drawn in the early 1820s, when the U.S. Army began establishing military forts along the waterways of the area, ostensibly for defense but also to encourage expansion to the West. These forts offered a form of protection to settlers, and their presence also helped register ownership of the land for the American government, while the military roads built to link the forts created more easily traveled transportation routes. As evidenced by extant land plans of the era, some soldiers maintained fort gardens, such as that of Fort Howard at the mouth of the Fox River, although the fort's main food and medicinal supplies were sent from headquarters on the East Coast.[4] In addition, military physicians like William Beaumont often grew medicinal plants, including hops and poppies, to supplement the army's Shaker-provided medicine.[5]

Yankee movement into the Northwest Territory continued to increase during the 1830s. The opening of the Erie Canal made the journey inland easier, and conditions for settlement—the final treaty settlements that deprived indigenous people of their rights and pushed them westward; the government land survey that began in 1833; and the opening of land sales offices in Mineral Point and Green Bay in 1834, and Milwaukee in 1839—were met.[6]

In 1836 Wisconsin achieved territorial status, and eastern seaboard land speculators and entrepreneurs eager to take advantage of the expanse of available land platted towns in grid patterns to encourage settlement. Wisconsin, like other states west of the Appalachians, was surveyed using the township and range system, which formed six-square-mile townships that were further divided into thirty-six individual sections. Section roads usually cross the landscape at right angles to each other with no modification for topography. Most early Wisconsin towns were platted according to a Cartesian grid system that further reinforced the geometric appearance of the Wisconsin cultural landscape. As a result, both rural and urban home grounds exhibited strong geometric components.

The Wisconsin Territory of 1840 incorporated a diverse landscape. Along the Lake Michigan shoreline and the bay of Green Bay, communities were already established near river mouths and natural harbors such as Green Bay, De Pere, and Sheboygan. The northern tier of the state was dominated by the dense white pine forest that had just begun to be opened up to the intense logging activity that would quickly decimate it. Settlements were sparse in this section and were mainly located in forest openings occupied by the Indians who had retreated there. The middle tier of the territory was composed of mixed boreal forest, which was fairly inaccessible, with the exception of the portage area between the Fox and Wisconsin rivers, where the town of Portage created a natural transportation hub.

A very different scene had emerged in the southeastern portion of the territory. This gentle terrain, with its many rivers and rich glacial topsoil, attracted Yankee pioneers who were eager to buy cheap land and establish communities. Rivers such as the Rock, Sugar, and Pecatonica provided waterpower to run the ubiquitous sawmills that were often the precursor of a community hub. Isolated farmsteads consisting of a few log buildings and fields in the process of being cleared for crops dotted the rural landscape. Of the thirty thousand people listed in the 1840 population census for the Wisconsin Territory, the majority were clustered in this area.[7] Most were Yankee pioneers who either had traveled directly from New England, New York, or Pennsylvania or had relocated from previously settled Midwestern states in search of inexpensive agricultural land.[8] Farther west, small clusters of rough dwellings marked the site of early mining communities such as Mineral Point, most stretching along the hillsides and valleys of the Driftless Area of the southwest.

After 1848, the year Wisconsin achieved statehood, the landscape changed dramatically as the new state began an aggressive campaign to attract northern Europeans with the promise of cheap land, favorable climatic conditions, voting rights, and other incentives. The result was a huge increase in the immigration of settlers who sought land in addition to religious, political, and economic freedom. By 1870 Wisconsin's population stood at more than one million, and progress in road and railroad construction had provided not only effective transportation routes for new settlers into the interior of the state but also the means to transport materials and goods from these areas to ports.

The largest immigrant ethnic group during this time period was from "Germany," which, until unification of the German Empire in 1871, was actually a group of independent states, including Pomerania, Bavaria, and Prussia. Their influence on the cultural landscape of Wisconsin, particularly the effects that their gardening methods and techniques had on the physical landscape, has been well documented. Other ethnic groups that accounted for Wisconsin's 1870 population growth came from Norway, Sweden, Denmark, Switzerland, Holland, and Belgium. Settlement spread outward from Milwaukee in a northwesterly direction, along river valleys and transportation routes.[9]

The result of increased immigration and settlement led to a change in the Wisconsin landscape, as farmland was carved from the wilderness. Wisconsin geographer Clarence W. Olmstead describes this as a "transitional" period, as farmers struggled to clear and improve the land for commercial crop production. He describes a typical rural landscape of the era as follows:

> [S]cattered, partly improved farms of perhaps 40–100 acres. Small irregular fields, enclosed by rail fences and worked by oxen, men, women and children produced wheat, corn, potatoes and subsidiary crops such as barley, rye or hemp. . . . [O]n older or better farms there would be a log or frame stable, corncrib, chicken coop, springhouse or other structures. An outdoor privy, a small garden and perhaps a patch of tobacco and a few fruit trees completed the farmstead.[10]

Olmstead continued by describing the small community hubs that emerged every few miles to provide basic needs—a blacksmith shop, general store, grist mills and sawmills, a school, and a church—but also stated:

> *It was a landscape in transition—unfinished, unkempt, and entirely utilitarian, with no frills or embellishments, except on the rare holdings of the wealthy, and those mainly in developing towns.*[11]

The transition between wilderness and domestication was at the foundation of the struggle that pioneers underwent as they strove to tame the land and make order out of "chaos."[12]

In Wisconsin, the difficulties of this transitional period were eased somewhat when the Wisconsin State Agricultural Society was formed in 1849 with the goal "to promote and improve the condition of Agriculture, Horticulture, and the Mechanical, Manufacturing, and Household Arts."[13] For isolated homesteaders, this organization likely provided much-needed encouragement as they cleared their land for crops and gardens.

As Yankee settlers moved westward in the early nineteenth century, they brought with them memories of the New England gardens they had left behind, and they were eager to re-create them in the unfamiliar landscape they encountered. A detailed study completed by landscape historian Sharon D. Crawford in the mid-1970s indicated that in the southern area of Wisconsin, the site of earliest Anglo-American settlement, the need for shelter and subsistence crops took priority. Potatoes and corn were the first crops to be planted in part because furrows and long rows could be used instead of plowing an entire field.[14] As land was cleared, grain crops were added, the most important of which was wheat. Crawford defined the style of early farm gardens as "pragmatic"—that is, gardens that were for survival rather than ornamentation.[15] Located close to the house, these gardens may have contained vegetables such as pumpkins, onions, cabbage, carrots, beets, and turnips, as well as a few medicinal or cooking herbs.

As Clarence W. Olmstead noted, small native fruit trees, such as wild plum and crab apple, were sometimes transplanted around the house, along with grape ivy that could be trained on a porch trellis. Crawford found little evidence of flower gardening in her research, concluding that it was not for lack of interest or aesthetic aptitude but because of lack of time, funds, and availability.[16] She noted that "the few settlers who had

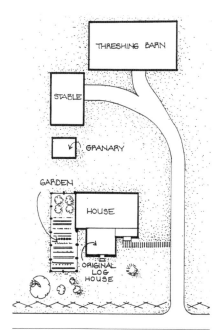

Above left: Early Wisconsin farmstead gardens were typically close to the house for ease of maintenance and harvesting.

ILLUSTRATION BY JEAN REINCE SCHWARTZ IN "THE DEVELOPMENT AND EVOLUTION OF DOMESTIC GARDENS IN SOUTHERN WISCONSIN DURING THE NINETEENTH CENTURY," 1983, COURTESY SHARON D. CRAWFORD

Above right: This re-created Danish settler garden at Old World Wisconsin confirms landscape historian Sharon D. Crawford's theory that pioneer gardens tended to be "pragmatic" in nature. Vegetables, herbs, and flowers are intermixed, close to the house.

LEE SOMERVILLE

brought shrubs, bulbs or flower seeds planted them, but diary entries lamenting the death of these first plants indicate that there was little time to coddle young plants until they were established."[17] Hardy shrubs such as lilac and perennials such as daylilies had a much better chance of survival and can often be seen to this day around old farmsteads.

Crawford found that this "pragmatic" garden was not linked to a particular time period, but rather was the product of early settlement. In southeastern Wisconsin this primarily occurred during the 1840s; in other parts of the state, European immigrant settlement continued until the turn of the twentieth century and beyond. According to Crawford, new settlers took an average of ten years to replace their log pioneer home with a more substantial brick, stone, or wood structure, and it usually was not until this time that more elaborate gardens were planned.[18] In southern Wisconsin, this occurred between the 1850s and the 1860s, when the increased availability of seeds and plants—either from local sources or itinerant peddlers—combined with the improved mail services that delivered mail-order seeds, magazines, and horticultural books changed the expectations that farmers and, to a greater degree, their wives had for their home gardens.[19]

Regionally, local nurseries, publications like *Western Farmer* (later *Wisconsin Farmer*), and organizations such as the Grange or Farmers' Institutes offered support and advice to Wisconsin residents, not only for farming but also for horticultural practices.[20] The Wisconsin State Agricultural Society meetings also provided opportunities for speakers to critique existing conditions and define their expectations for the improvement of home grounds. At the 1853 meeting, speaker Laura Smith vividly described a rural farmstead that she claimed "we too often behold" in the countryside:

> *It is a log-house, and a stick-chimney; upon one side, in full view of the cabin's one door and window, is a log barn, and the cows and pigs make a common bed in front of the house; old boxes, barrels, refuse wood, chips, etc., add confusion to the scene; no tree has been spared, though numerous blackened stumps too truly indicate where once they waved in leafy pride. A few straggling stalks of mustard, possibly a tall sunflower, some thistles—introduced from Canada—and burdocks, flourish in the yard. Perhaps, the good wife has planted in a plowed patch near by, a few onions and cabbages; all, indeed, wears a most comfortless and uninviting aspect.*[21]

Crawford defined the expanded gardens that began to appear in rural southern Wisconsin in the 1850s as "traditional" in that they contained elements of New England dooryard gardens and the English cottage garden:

> *A common characteristic was a straight front walk leading from the gate to the front door of the house. . . . Dirt paths and flower beds were frequently defined by a neat edging of stones or boards. Pairs of trees or shrubs were often positioned symmetrically on opposite sides of the gate, but the symmetrical effect was seldom carried all the way back to the house.*[22]

The appearance of lawns, seeded with imported grasses and cut with a scythe or grazed periodically, was more apparent by the early 1860s. Often the area immediately around the home was enclosed with a fence to protect the vegetable and flower beds from wandering farm animals and to separate the flower and vegetable gardens from farm fields or pasture.

Shrubs, trees, and fruit bushes could be purchased from itinerant peddlers and local nurseries or simply transplanted from the wild. Yet, even with available literature on garden design, Crawford concluded, nostalgia and folk knowledge determined the appearance of the garden, which she called a "frontier adaptation of an ancient gardening tradition."[23]

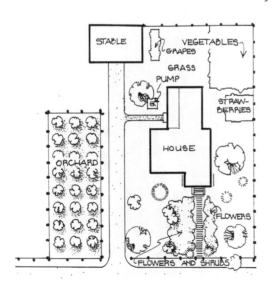

Crawford's "traditional" garden: As was typical of these gardens that appeared about a decade after settlement, it contains an established orchard, a vegetable garden behind the house, and a boardwalk lined with shrubs and flowers.

ILLUSTRATION BY JEAN REINCE SCHWARTZ IN "THE DEVELOPMENT AND EVOLUTION OF DOMESTIC GARDENS IN SOUTHERN WISCONSIN DURING THE NINETEENTH CENTURY," 1983, COURTESY SHARON D. CRAWFORD

This circa 1875 Andreas Larsen Dahl photograph illustrates the type of garden Crawford described as "traditional." The family has spilled over into the perennial beds lining the pathway to the front of the house. Iris, lilies, and peony bushes frame the pathway, with larger shrubs to the rear of the beds.
WHI IMAGE ID 26771

❧ ANDREAS LARSEN DAHL ❧

Andreas Larsen Dalen, 1844–1923, emigrated from his hometown of Valdres in Norway to join his brother Nels in DeForest, Wisconsin, in 1869. He changed his surname to Dahl and quickly established a business as a "daguerrian artist."[1] For the next ten years, he spent the summer months traveling around the Dane County area by horse and buggy, hauling his photographic equipment with him and taking pictures of families. During the winter he worked in his darkroom, then returned to sell the prints he had made so they could be sent to relatives back home as a document of the immigrants' new lives.

The series of Dahl photographs reproduced here underscores the pride that immigrant families felt in their accomplishments in the New World. Generations of family members sit or stand, often with their prized possessions, framed by their home and garden. Many of Dahl's subjects are of Norwegian origin, but he did not limit his photography to one ethnic group.

These archival photographs are an invaluable source for students of Wisconsin cultural history because they illustrate vernacular architecture, material culture, and family structure. However, they are also an important documentation of garden history.

The home of Samuel Barber, the Middleton depot manager, circa 1873. Notice the decorative fencing and house trim, and the number of small shrubs and trees edging the lawn in the front yard.

WHI IMAGE ID 26971

❧ ANDREAS LARSEN DAHL ❧

Left: Few improvements have yet been made to the yard of this isolated farmhouse, circa 1872. The carpenter's saw in the foreground may be a clue that construction of the house was either very recent or ongoing. WHI IMAGE ID 26765

Right: The newly planted trees indicate that this circa 1869 garden is also in the development stage. WHI IMAGE ID 26973

Despite the different layouts of the gardens, certain common themes are evident. For example, most include straight pathways, either of dirt or boardwalks; raised beds; a variety of annual and perennial plants; and deciduous and evergreen trees including apple, birch, poplar, and cedar. Dahl also captured evidence of street planting and a wide variety of fencing design and material in his photographs.

In 1879, after a serious illness, Dahl decided to enter the seminary. He put his camera away and spent the rest of his life as a Lutheran minister, leaving his glass slides in a barn that belonged to his brother.

In 1976 they were found and donated to the Wisconsin Historical Society. They provide a significant and extraordinary historical record of the homes, culture, and landscapes of a group of immigrants who otherwise would have been forgotten.[2]

NOTES

1. David Mandel, *Settlers of Dane County* (Madison: Dane County Cultural Commission, 1985), 9.

2. Dahl's photographs are available for viewing on the Wisconsin Historical Society website: http://www.wisconsinhistory.org.

ANDREAS LARSEN DAHL

Poplar trees are planted inside the fence and lilac bushes on each side of the front door, circa 1872. Like peonies, the lilac bush was typically a garden favorite of newly arrived settlers. It was easy to start from cuttings, quick to grow, and provided fragrance and beauty with little effort. WHI IMAGE ID 27007

This Greek Revival home is tentatively identified as schoolteacher Carla Burten's residence in Black Earth, circa 1872. The exuberantly planted yard contains a mix of peonies, daisies, and other flowers in beds that extend from the house to the fence. Small evergreen shrubs have been planted close to the house, while thriving maple trees line the far fence. WHI IMAGE ID 27004

Opposite page, clockwise from top left: There has been little attempt to beautify the wooded yard of this unknown family, circa 1869. The table may have been brought down from the front porch, which, with its potted plants and birdcages, provided a comfortable outdoor seating area. WHI IMAGE ID 27055

This family portrait was taken in Pleasant Springs, circa 1874. A straight board pathway with slightly raised beds on each side leads directly to the front porch. The garden includes an apple tree and several peonies, among other flowers. WHI IMAGE ID 27057

An unpainted picket fence encloses and separates the front garden of the Henry Hooker family's Springfield home from the farmyard, circa 1871. Vines, probably morning glories, climb the fence and low shrubs form a foundation planting along the front wall of the home. WHI IMAGE ID 27090

❧ ANDREAS LARSEN DAHL ❧

Having studied the Andreas Larsen Dahl photographs, Crawford found a wide variation in the appearance of Dane County gardens: some showed wide lawns and neat beds edging pathways, while others were filled entirely with flower beds. Crawford noted that Wisconsin State Horticultural Society authors did not approve of this type of "old-fashioned" garden, calling it confusing and weedy; they much preferred wide swaths of lawn with bedding plants contained in beds cut into the lawn.[24]

Patterns for complicated cutout beds were included in most American horticultural and garden books, but Crawford found that the high cost of upkeep made them impractical for most Wisconsin gardeners; a simpler plan was to cut a single round bed into the lawn and fill it with an exotic-looking plant such as the canna lily. This type of bed can still be seen in farmstead lawns.[25]

According to Clarence W. Olmstead, the period between 1870 and 1920 was a time of consolidation for Wisconsin agriculture.[26] The pioneer farmer had, generally speaking, been self-sufficient, producing enough crops to feed his family and a few animals. The pattern on the western frontier in Wisconsin and beyond was that wheat would serve as the first commercial crop. Typically, after a few years, disease and soil depletion caused a decline in wheat production, necessitating diversification into other crop or animal production. In Wisconsin, dairy farming emerged as an attractive alternative, strongly encouraged by a group of New York dairymen who had relocated to Madison in the late 1860s.

As farmers increased the size of their dairy herds, creameries and cheese factories were needed within easy distance for the surplus milk. These tended to be located at natural hubs, such as crossroads, and at regular intervals, usually about three miles apart. The previously isolated and self-sufficient farmer now delivered his milk to a community gathering place that often included a general store, a blacksmith shop, and sometimes a school, in addition to the cheese factory. The introduction of silos meant that cattle could be fed and milked year-round, thereby necessitating the construction of dairy barns. Olmstead noted that the landscape was significantly changed:

[T]he process of creating a human-dominant landscape out of wilderness was essentially completed. In 1870, about half the land was in farms; by 1920, virtually all was transformed. Not only did people bring most of the land into use, they also

Opposite page:
The brick Dane County farm home of Halvor Nerison Hauge, circa 1868. Dahl posed the family inside the fence used to protect the garden from the cattle in the surrounding fields.
WHI IMAGE ID 1986

Photographed by Dahl circa 1872, this garden illustrates the exuberant use of flowers in the front and side yards. The family stands near a group of potted plants that might have been moved outside for the summer. Identifying individual plants from these photographs is sometimes impossible, but the flowers in the foreground appear to be a type of daisy.

WHI IMAGE ID 26655

Crawford found evidence of what she called "Victorian" elements in southern Wisconsin gardens in the last quarter of the nineteenth century, including carpet beds cut into the lawn, specimen trees and shrubs dotting the lawn area, and curved driveways.

ILLUSTRATION BY JEAN REINCE SCHWARTZ IN "THE DEVELOPMENT AND EVOLUTION OF DOMESTIC GARDENS IN SOUTHERN WISCONSIN DURING THE NINETEENTH CENTURY," 1983, COURTESY SHARON D. CRAWFORD

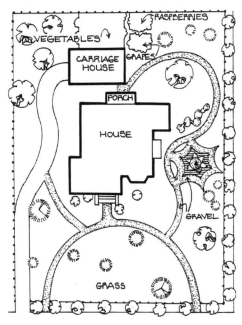

changed the kinds of use, especially the system of farming, thereby creating new ensembles of features—new landscapes.[27]

Wisconsin's urban landscape was also undergoing significant change during this period. European immigration, which had slowed during the post–Civil War economic depression, swelled once more, as immigrants from southern and eastern European countries entered the industrial workforce primarily centered in the southeastern portion of the state.

Against this background of change, the rural Wisconsin vernacular garden also evolved. Crawford found evidence of what she defined as "Victorian" elements in post–Civil War southern Wisconsin vernacular gardens. Typically they included large expanses of lawn with clumps of trees and shrubs around the perimeter; the use of weeping varieties of trees as specimen plants; cutout beds; trellises and arbors supporting vines; decorative small buildings such as gazebos and garden houses; curving pathways; and, among the wealthier households, conservatories and greenhouses. The Mitchell home described in chapter 3 is a good example of the high-style interpretation of this fashion in an urban landscape.

By 1870 some 25 percent of the Wisconsin population was of German origin; their influence on all aspects of community life cannot be ignored.[28] A 2002 study done by historian James William Miller for the three German settler gardens at Old World Wisconsin traces the transition of the appearance and contents of the German peasant garden from its medieval origins to late-nineteenth-century Wisconsin.[29]

According to Miller, peasant gardens in the German-speaking states contrasted with those established by immigrants from other European countries, displaying elements that were more closely related to medieval monastery gardens. Laid out in a geometric, sometimes cruciform, shape, these gardens were divided into equal areas by pathways and a central open space that often contained a well. Beds rather than rows were used; sometimes these were raised and bordered with wood or stone.

The establishment of a large kitchen garden was, Miller noted, a higher priority for German immigrants than other groups and was the responsibility of the housewife alone: its placement in front of the house advertised her industriousness and success to passersby. Changes in German American gardens during the acculturation period of the mid- to late 1800s included the use of both bed and row gardens and the relocation of the garden from the front to the side of the home, which highlighted the decreasing importance of the garden as a symbol of women's industriousness and as a sole source for food.

Miller and others claim that since the diet of the German-speaking people contained more vegetables than those of other European countries, especially England, where

meat was considered more important, the German garden contained many more varieties and numbers of vegetables. Since many of these varieties were unavailable in this country in the 1860s, seeds were brought in by new immigrants or mailed from the Old Country.[30] Both Miller and Crawford mention the importance of German immigrant seed dealers in the United States, including James Vick of Rochester, New York, who, by 1870, was advertising extensively in German American newspapers. In Wisconsin, Adolf Meissner's seed company supplied many German varieties to immigrants.[31]

German immigration decreased during the 1890s, but Wisconsin remained a popular destination for other European emigrants until about 1920. According to geographer Robert Ostergren, this "final phase" of settlement consisted mainly of immigrants from eastern and southern Europe who either "filled in" the available land in less than ideal farming areas in the northwestern part of the state or moved directly into industrial hubs like Racine or Milwaukee, where job availability was high.[32] The towns along rail, road, and river corridors through the interior of the state were also populated during this period, often by settlers who relocated from southeastern Wisconsin. By 1920 about half of Wisconsin's three million residents lived in urban areas—almost one-third of them in Milwaukee.

Like the Germans, each group brought its own methods of farming and gardening practices with them. Joseph Schafer, author of the 1922 publication *A History of Agriculture in Wisconsin*, remembered significant differences between what he called "American" and "immigrant" rural gardens:

> *Every foreign element had its own peculiar customs both inside the home and outside. In cookery they introduced new dishes, in gardening new plants and new varieties of flowers. Germans, Scandinavians, Bohemians and others were wedded to gardening as a feature of home making. Some Americans also were excellent gardeners, but many of them were content to raise a few things only, like early potatoes, some cabbages and melons. With the foreigners gardening was a household art. The women and younger children performed the labor, and the gardens—a small plot of ground next the house, highly fertilized, cultivated extensively, fenced against poultry by means of either pickets or woven willows— was apt to be a charming little world with its plats separated by lily bordered paths growing scores of different esculents, its currant and gooseberry bushes lining the fence, and its clusters of decorative flowers, shrubs, and vines. Perhaps there was also a "summer house" of lattice work covered with morning-glory. Though the houses*

of immigrants might be inferior to those of their American neighbors, their gardens, which guests were always glad to visit, compensated them in large measure.[33]

The national social reform movement that occurred around the turn of the twentieth century also affected the landscape of Wisconsin, as is evidenced in the change in population distribution; the continuing growth of agricultural, industrial, and commercial centers in major cities; and improved transportation routes throughout the state. Civic improvement organizations in Wisconsin were as active as those in other states. In most cases they were founded and run by women who belonged to local clubs coordinated at the state level by the Wisconsin Federation of Women's Clubs, which had a membership of 131 clubs and 5,200 clubwomen in 1900.[34] The Woman's Club of Madison, originally formed as a social and literary outlet for wives of professional men, developed into an active civic reform group that worked on several different projects each year, including playground and school improvement. In conjunction with the Madison Park and Pleasure Association, they organized a "Town Improvement" campaign that encouraged homeowners to sign agreements to keep their yards and gardens clean and tidy.[35]

Against this backdrop, the Wisconsin State Horticultural Society emerged as an important source of horticultural information and support for professional and amateur horticulturists as well as the Wisconsin homeowner.

The Pleasures and Benefits
of Amateur Horticulture

[O]ur whole wide west will yet be clothed with beauty and excellence, as
"with a garment," and first among her sister states shall be our own Wisconsin.
Her own peculiar climate shall yield its own peculiar fruit, and beautiful
homes, with splendid trees and clustering vines, and fragrant flowers shall
everywhere adorn her prairies and her woodlands.

MRS. D. HUNTLEY, 1873[1]

Nineteenth-century Wisconsin gardens, like all gardens, had their individual nature. The diverse groups of immigrants and easterners who settled the state brought with them their cultural traditions and history, which they adapted over time to the very different landscapes, soils, and climate of the region.

For some, the Wisconsin State Horticultural Society was a practical and significant source of information. Through its publications and meetings, the organization attempted to reach these isolated pioneers as they built their homes and communities in a new and unknown environment. The society developed a broad-based home horticultural support program for its members in addition to its primary mission of providing the practical research to advance the state's commercial fruit industry. The contents of the society's annual reports and journals provide not only a fascinating history of the organization but

SUMMER MEETING

ON THE LAWN AT MENDOTA BEACH

Wisconsin State Horticultural Society members lunching on the banks of Lake Mendota, 1915. The gentleman with the white beard in the foreground is William Toole. *WISCONSIN HORTICULTURE, SEPTEMBER 1915*

also invaluable documentation about the changing philosophy regarding the significance of gardens and gardening to Wisconsin residents. The articles, meeting presentations, local society reports, and proceedings of annual business meetings offer the modern reader an array of interesting topics that illustrate the changing guidelines and recommendations for the improvement of Wisconsin home grounds.

In 1869 WSHS dues were set at $1 per year or $5 for a lifetime. Many early members were already active in local horticultural societies, such as those in Madison, Kenosha, Oshkosh, Janesville, and Grant County; some of these members became early board members of the society.[2] Annual meetings were held in Madison in February, with additional business meetings held in conjunction with the Wisconsin State Agricultural Society during the Wisconsin State Fair in August. The complete proceedings of winter and summer meetings were recorded, transcribed, and printed as *Transactions of the Wisconsin State Horticultural Society*, which was renamed *Annual Report of the Wisconsin State Horticultural Society* in 1890. Bound copies were distributed to members of the society, members of the Wisconsin legislature, public libraries, and other organizations.

Membership rolls were published annually until 1910, when the list became unwieldy.

In 1869 the membership stood at thirty-five; this number increased to four hundred by 1900 and to twenty-five hundred by 1915. By 1928 there were close to three thousand members.[3] Though names on early membership lists indicate a preponderance of Anglo-Americans, by 1910 the membership appears to have become more ethnically diverse.[4]

While most members in the 1870s lived within a fifty-mile radius of Madison, statewide representation gradually increased over the next several years, probably as a result of such factors as improved rail and road transportation networks; the rise of commercial apple production in the northern and western portions of the state; and an increasing number of horticultural societies affiliated with the WSHS. By 1910 most counties were represented in the membership list, with the largest number of members in Dane, Milwaukee, Bayfield, Walworth, and Winnebago counties.[5]

Between 1869 and 1928, sixty *Transactions* or *Annual Reports* were published. WSHS members also received the monthly edition of *The Wisconsin Horticulturist* between 1896 and 1903. After *The Wisconsin Horticulturist* was discontinued, the WSHS distributed bulletins on an as-needed basis; however, these were no longer issued after the society decided to produce a much larger, more inclusive, and ultimately more

Wisconsin Horticulture was issued on a monthly basis by the WSHS between 1910 and 1967. This March 1913 edition was typical in that it contained a miscellany of useful information for the Wisconsin orchardist and gardener.

WISCONSIN HORTICULTURE

OFFICIAL ORGAN OF THE WISCONSIN STATE HORTICULTURAL SOCIETY

Volume III   Madison, Wisconsin, March, 1913   **Number 7**

Hardy Perennials for Wisconsin

WM. A. TOOLE.

Of late years there has been a steadily increasing interest in perennials for the home flower garden, or as an addition to the shrubbery border. While they do not give the showy bedding effects of geraniums for the whole summer, there is a wide variety in form and color and a succession of bloom may be had from early spring to late fall. Most of them are superior for cutting. Many of them are decorative in foliage before or after the blossoming time. All of them are desirable because they do not need replanting every year. It is a mistake to assume that because they live from year to year, that no further care is required after planting out. To get good results they need cultivation the same as any plant. To successfully winter many of them over it is necessary to prevent seed production.

There are three of the hardy perennials that are so popular and may be had in such wide variety that separate talks are needed for each of them. These are peonies, iris and perennial phlox.

grown plants in the fall during September or October. Mulch heavily each fall with stable manure. Rake off the coarsest in the spring but leave the balance as fertilizer. When the plants get quite large and old,

professional journal, *Wisconsin Horticulture*. From 1910 until 1967, this publication was sent to members monthly.

Between 1869 and 1928 about 80 percent of the presentations at any one WSHS meeting related to the commercial fruit-growing industry—which followed WSHS's stated primary mission of promoting and advancing the development of the Wisconsin fruit industry.[6] The "advancement of the art of horticulture"—the second objective of the WSHS—was addressed in several ways, the most obvious being the inclusion of meeting topics that related to the improvement and beautification of home grounds. Usually, two or three papers on this subject—with such titles as "Rural Homes" (Mrs. D. Huntley, 1873), "Trees and Foliage in Landscape" (Charles S. Abbott, 1876), "Horticulture on the Farm" (A. A. Arnold, 1878), or "The Farmer's Dooryard" (Mrs. D. Huntley, 1879)—were presented at each meeting.[7]

Indirectly related topics were sometimes introduced under the WSHS's banner of the "advancement of the art of horticulture." Social reform was in the national spotlight during this period, and by promoting the return to a simpler lifestyle idealized as a love for nature, the garden, and children, Wisconsin horticulturists were following a national trend. The WSHS annual meetings were a useful platform for speakers, both men and women, to introduce their concerns about the developing problems of an increasingly urban world. While these presentations may not have directly addressed the vernacular garden or its contents, they provide cultural context and background for the changes in the appearance and composition of home grounds.

Before the turn of the twentieth century, the WSHS meetings appear to have simply provided platforms for individual members to publicize their particular beliefs, which often echoed their religious or ethical convictions. Their recommendations for "the beautification of home grounds" symbolically represented the speakers' eagerness to improve the moral and ethical standards in the home and community. Vivid descriptions of cluttered, weed-covered farmsteads or dirty city streets were usually followed by pleas for cleaner, more ordered home and city landscapes, with the implication that family and community contentment would result. In this respect, WSHS meetings were typical of the format of other horticultural societies: historian Tamara Plakins Thornton, writing about horticulture and the American character, described them as "orgies of self-congratulation."[8]

Speakers tended to be verbose and subjective, with noticeable spiritual, religious, moralistic, sentimental, and sometimes sexist overtones to their themes. The following example from an 1871 paper by H. W. Roby, entitled "Pleasures and Benefits of Amateur Florticulture," epitomizes the type of oratory that was practiced by some members during the early years of society operation:

> *If the ladies of our cities would give as much time and attention to the adornment of their homes and flower-gardens as they spend in worrying over the sickly whims and fancies of having the finest and most stylish turnout, the grandest and most dazzling equipage in the city, their physical and moral tone would be as much improved as their homes and gardens; and their doctors and druggists' bills for prescriptions, stimulants and cosmetics would be very much reduced. If, instead of the (sometimes bitter) rivalry between neighboring ladies as to whose establishment should be the most gaudy, their rivalry were turned into that exhilarating emulation as to whose flower garden should be the most resplendent and beautiful, that morbid, deathly palor, so observable upon our streets and in public gatherings, would be dispelled, and the rose-bloom of health and true hilarity would supplant it. And, if they would spend as much time and money in cultivating flowers, as they do in buying and reading trashy and corrupting literature, their health, their morals and their stock of useful information would be greatly improved.*[9]

While most male speakers did not vent as vehemently as did Mr. Roby, and in fact were usually solicitous of their female speakers and audience members, there is an underlying thread, typical of the era, that women were fragile in mind and body and should therefore be protected from physical labor—this, despite the fact that on the pioneer farmstead, women of all ethnic backgrounds did their share of physical work, whether in the barnyard, kitchen, or farm field. In 1872 Henry T. Williams recognized the contributions of women on the landscape:

> *Bless the ladies! for to them we owe more than half the interest in elegant or tasteful home surroundings; and I sincerely believe at the present day, if we wish to extend the good work of rural taste, let us first talk to the ladies.*[10]

Although nothing in the WSHS constitution and bylaws specifically barred women from joining the society, it was not until 1884 that women were listed as full members.[11] Prior to that date, women presenters at annual meetings had been granted an honorary annual membership. Published membership lists continued to show a very low percentage of women members; most of the women involved were wives or daughters of male members. However, it is interesting to note that in 1884, Mrs. Charlotte Lewis, a frequent contributor at the annual meetings, was appointed secretary.[12]

Women were fairly regular contributors at the annual meetings, although they often prefaced their presentations with apologies for their limited knowledge and experience. Poetry and religious references were plentiful, and the secondary status of women in society seemed to be generally accepted by both sexes. For example, "Mrs. Prof. A. Kerr," speaking at the 1880 annual meeting in Madison, opined the following:

> Now I would not have you imagine for a moment . . . that a woman should do all
> the work in her garden. A woman has no right to make herself a household drudge,
> indoors or out. She is queen of the kingdom of home, and, "with love's invisible
> scepter laden," she may rule the hearts of those who rule the world.[13]

It is interesting to trace the changes that occurred over the course of the next twenty years. From the women's presentations, it is clear that they were developing more confidence in their roles as speakers. While floriculture remained a popular topic, some women, including Charlotte Lewis, introduced deeper social issues, such as the difficulties of isolated farm life, the rationale for women's suffrage, the disgraceful state of rural schoolhouses, and a host of other topics that were gradually incorporated into civic improvement projects, often led by the very women who had been early members of the WSHS. One of these activists and a regular contributor at the annual meetings was Mrs. Vie H. Campbell from Evansville, who, in 1896, became the assistant editor of *The Wisconsin Horticulturist*; her position was short-lived, however, apparently because of some disagreement concerning the amount of poetry and literature she wanted to include in the journal.[14] In February 1897 Mary C. C. Johnson (Mrs. Franklin Johnson) of Baraboo became the sole editor, a position she held for two years. Fifteen years later the "Gardens" section of *Wisconsin Horticulture* was edited entirely by women: the subheading noted that it was a "department conducted by practical women who really have gardens." The WSHS established a Women's Auxiliary in 1920; in 1928, part of this group founded the Wisconsin Garden Club Federation, which subsequently separated from the WSHS.

⚘ FREDERIC CRANEFIELD ⚘

Frederic Cranefield was a Fitchburg, Wisconsin, native who attended the University of Wisconsin and then became an assistant to Professor Emmet S. Goff in the school's Department of Horticulture.[1] Cranefield was an instructor in the department between 1897 and 1905, and he accepted the newly created position of executive secretary of the Wisconsin State Horticultural Society in 1904. For the next twenty-two years he not only managed the administrative duties of the position but was also influential in virtually all areas of the organization. He initiated reforms in the commercial apple industry that had far-reaching consequences in the success of the statewide venture, helped coordinate the Wisconsin war garden movement during American involvement in World War I, and was the first editor of *Wisconsin Horticulture*, which he founded in 1910. His tireless interest in promoting amateur horticulture throughout the state is evident in the content of the reports he provided at annual meetings. As editor of *Wisconsin Horticulture*, he strongly encouraged input from members, promising to "answer all questions," and wrote interesting editorials that dealt with statewide issues, often prompting responses from readers.[2] His landmark article "The Improvement of Home Grounds" was just one of the articles and editorials he authored during his tenure.[3]

NOTES

1. "Frederic Cranefield, Long Ill, Dies at 73," *The* (Wisconsin) *Capital Times*, 1939, n.d.

2. Frederic Cranefield, "To My Readers," *Wisconsin Horticulture* 17, no. 3 (November 1926), 34.

3. Frederic Cranefield, "The Improvement of Home Grounds," *Annual Report of the Wisconsin State Horticultural Society* 34 (1904), 264–302.

In 1904 Frederic Cranefield, a horticulturist with a strong academic background, was hired as the first executive secretary of the WSHS. This marked the start of a new era for the society, for he immediately instigated a more academic and much less subjective approach to both pomology and horticulture. He later credited Emmet S. Goff, director of the Department of Horticulture at the University of Wisconsin, and Madison banker Samuel Marshall for helping the WSHS "turn the corner" to become a more businesslike, contemporary, and professional organization.[15]

Cranefield encouraged members to continue and advance their existing outreach efforts in the burgeoning civic improvement movement. The topic had first been introduced to members in 1886, when a "selected contribution" entitled "Planting a School Ground" was included in the *Transactions*. The author "O. C. Simmons from

Michigan Horticulturist"—probably Ossian Cole Simonds, who later gained prominence as a proponent of the emerging Prairie School of landscape architecture—suggested gathering and planting native species of trees, vines, and plants around the perimeter of the schoolyard, leaving a neat lawn in the center.[16]

School grounds improvement became a recurring theme at meetings over the next several years, especially after Arbor Day was proclaimed in Wisconsin in 1889.[17] In a letter to the state superintendent of schools in 1891, the WSHS secretary suggested a format for the celebration in schools, including children's planting opportunities, with the WSHS donating plants and seeds.[18] The society also donated $1,000 in prize money to be distributed to the schools showing the greatest improvement in landscaping the grounds over the previous year.[19]

As part of its commitment to civic improvement, the WSHS strongly supported the formation of village and town improvement and horticultural societies, first described in a presentation by Emmet S. Goff.[20] Whether related to this appeal or not, the number of local horticultural societies in the state increased from just four in 1869 to thirty in 1910 and thirty-nine by 1928.[21]

Civic improvement topics reached a new level of popularity at annual meetings in 1914, when the WSHS began a unified effort to organize public and private "war gardens" for vegetable production. The danger of food shortages was a nationwide concern as the United States prepared to enter World War I. That year, war gardens were established on empty lots in Milwaukee, Madison, and Oshkosh. Members of civic groups as well as WSHS members, including many women, joined forces to educate and help residents construct and maintain these gardens, which resembled the traditional allotments commonly seen in more densely populated English cities. Reports at WSHS annual meetings indicated that this was a successful endeavor; after 1918 war gardens were renamed "victory gardens" in commemoration of the Allied victory and continued in existence with the help of WSHS volunteers at least until the mid-1940s. During the war years the WSHS and the Extension Office of the University of Wisconsin College of Agriculture published seven "War Garden Circulars" that were combined and reissued in 1919 as a twenty-page pamphlet entitled "Plant a Victory Garden"; in 1922 they were published as *The Wisconsin Garden Book*, authored by "Wisconsin Gardeners."[22]

As a result, pleasure gardening took a backseat for several years. In fact, after America's entry into World War I, an announcement in the April 1917 issue of *Wisconsin Horticulture* urged that home adornment be postponed as it might interfere with food production.[23] It was not until the mid-1920s that the topic of the layout of home grounds was revived, possibly as a result of several policy changes adopted by the membership in January 1925 to vigorously pursue statewide development of interest in ornamental planting, encourage growth and development of local horticultural societies and garden clubs, and actively seek a more inclusive membership. These policy changes seemed to have displeased the commercial growers, who retaliated by forcing Frederic Cranefield to resign as executive secretary. In a newspaper interview, Cranefield stated that he had been forced out because of his decision to use WSHS state-appropriated funds to advance amateur horticulture rather than allocate it to the commercial fruit industry.[24] This apparently caused a rift within the society: by the following year, WSHS amateur horticulturists, many of them women members, had decided to form the Wisconsin Garden Club Federation, which, although it retained affiliation with the WSHS, organized separate meeting and program venues.[25] By 1930, with the earlier formation of other small-interest groups such as the Wisconsin Beekeepers' Association, the Wisconsin Nurserymen's Association, and the Wisconsin Gladiolus Society, the WSHS had become primarily the voice of the commercial grower.[26]

The major patterns and trends of the WSHS recommendations for the home landscape can be traced throughout its publications from 1869 to 1928. These generally followed the national trend of a gradual movement away from the formal designs espoused by mid- to late-nineteenth-century American designers toward a more natural-appearing landscape that connected the home to the garden.

In 1869, as the WSHS was reorganizing after the Civil War, President Joseph Hobbins forcefully outlined the prevailing ideals for the vernacular garden in his opening address to the membership. His vivid and detailed description is relevant because it is one of the first written examples of the normative views of this group as it launched its vision for the future of horticulture in Wisconsin. The picture Hobbins painted can be clearly traced to the principles espoused by Andrew Jackson Downing, Jacob Weidenmann, Frank J. Scott, and others. Specific rules addressed the careful placement of trees, shrubs, and flower beds to create an ornamental front yard that would enhance the view from the

Featured in the 1872 *Transactions of the Wisconsin State Horticultural Society*, this lithograph of the Alexander Mitchell estate in Milwaukee was accompanied by a detailed description of the estate gardens that reportedly included more than 5,000 annuals. WHI IMAGE ID 80840

street and provide a picture for those inside the house. Boundary and edge elements were to be strongly defined to provide a pleasing geometric, though not necessarily symmetrical, pattern. Neatness, order, and beauty, Hobbins noted, were obtained by subduing and taming nature, so as to produce a tasteful result:

> [T]he first and greatest law of garden making. It must be pleasant . . . [and] to be pleasant, it must be made beautiful. Nothing unsightly must be seen. Nature must be won by art to mould herself to your taste and design, and the work being completed, the only test, a simple and ever true one of its perfection, is the spontaneous pleasure it gives to the intelligent eye. . . . The cultivated eye is the sole judge.
>
> A garden . . . is but a horticultural painting. . . . It should have its little lawn, its roses and honeysuckles on each side of the front door of your house, and its ivy, the Virginia creeper at each end of the piazza, and reaching as high as the chamber window and falling in graceful festoons from the house gables. It should have a variety of flowering shrubs, choice and increasing in size toward the dividing fence on one side and a moderate sized tree or two, ranged with a few evergreens on the other side, serving both for ornament and as a screen from the public gaze to the back garden. Make a little bed of perpetual roses and another for geraniums and verbenas, and intersperse a few hardy perennial plants among your shrubs. Plant a row of trees outside of your sidewalk, and the arrangements for the front of the house are tolerably complete. . . .
>
> I do not make it essential to have fountains, grotto work, statuary, or glass houses which will come with the coming wealth of the state, but rather address myself to what can be done now, with but little expense and with no more care than is at once pleasurable and profitable. . . . Individual taste, intelligence, experience and necessity will teach how this is to be done, and where these fail, this society will be found the best teacher.[27]

Hobbins's word painting would have been greatly enhanced with an accompanying illustration, but artwork was not usually included in the *Transactions*, likely because of the expense. However, on three occasions between 1872 and 1878, a frontispiece image was incorporated into the published proceedings, and each one supports the ideals Hobbins was promoting.

One example included in the 1872 *Transactions* accompanied a detailed report of a tour through the home and gardens of the newly completed Alexander Mitchell house on Spring Street in Milwaukee. The lithograph shows the massive Italianate mansion

A Downing-type Gothic
Revival cottage was the
frontispiece for the 1873
Transactions. No detail is
given in the text, but the
appearance of the cottage
and its neat landscape
indicates that the WSHS
was using it as an example
of "what to do."

The frontispiece for the 1878 *Transactions* exemplifies the orderly arrangement of an idealized farmstead. No source for this lithograph appears in the text.

EVERGREEN SHELTER BELTS AND ORNAMENTAL HEDGES.

surrounded by formal lawns and ornate outbuildings. An iron fence encloses the city-block-sized estate, allowing passersby a view of the sweeping driveways, glass conservatories, formal beds of annuals, and single specimen trees placed in large expanses of lawn. The lithograph does not show the thirty-three carpet beds described in the accompanying text as containing more than five thousand annual plants. Also described are numerous plant houses for vines, eight hundred varieties of roses, pineapples, tropical specimen plants, and nurseries. Mrs. Alexander Mitchell and her gardener, Joseph Pollard, were credited with designing and maintaining this magnificent estate. Not surprisingly, Mrs. Mitchell was often listed as an award winner at the state fair flower show. The Mitchell estate was by no means a vernacular garden, but it was obviously eye-catching and exemplified the formal elements and grandeur of the latest fashions in an 1870s high-style garden.

A second frontispiece, included in the 1873 *Transactions*, was probably a more realistic model for the Wisconsin gardener. It featured a small but decorative Downing-type gothic cottage framed by a well-kept, restrained home garden. The paths and a small round bed are neatly edged with rows of plants, and a larger bed of perennial flowers adds a vertical element.

The frontispiece of the 1878 *Transactions* depicted an unnamed prosperous rural farmstead with strong geometric elements in the architecture and landscape, which are emphasized by the surrounding hedges and shelterbelts. The ornamental parterre garden, separate vegetable plot, curved pathways, and specimen trees are reminiscent of the 1870 Weidenmann designs (see pages 4–5). The inclusion of this lithograph in the *Transactions* serves as another indication that Wisconsin horticulturists were following the national trends of formality and order in the landscape.

As in other parts of the country, the Wisconsin home garden was gradually changing in appearance and function. Rather than a merely decorative frame for the house, the garden was becoming an outdoor living room where family members could work and play together. In 1904 Frederic Cranefield summed up the prevailing WSHS principles, clearly referring to the symbolic relationship between a pleasant garden and a pleasant life:

> *A well kept lawn with shade trees, flowering plants and vines will unconsciously develop in the child's mind a love of home and of the beautiful in nature that may in later years repay many fold the expense involved, while bare and cheerless surroundings will engender a feeling of discontent as well as a lessened capability to appreciate the refinements of life.*[28]

By this time the WSHS was increasingly focused on the layout and improvement of village, urban, and suburban home grounds, rather than its earlier emphasis on the rural farmstead. WSHS speakers were also strongly promoting the use of native plants in the home landscape.

Although beauty was still considered to be a guiding principle in garden design by 1930, the "cultivated eye" that Hobbins mentioned saw the garden differently. No longer just admired from afar, the garden had developed into a habitable living space to be used for work, play, and relaxation. Individual expression and personal participation were, according to the following excerpt from a *Wisconsin Horticulture* article, now considered more important than outdated traditions:

> *In garden design there are traditions and conventions. Methods of arranging plants in gardens have been generally accepted in different countries at different periods, and these methods have become traditional. . . . But now the tendency is to disregard traditions and conventions. . . . In designing a garden, one merely arranges flowers and plants, so that they make a beautiful picture, and a picture of a kind that one*

The placement of Wychwood, the Lake Geneva home of the Hutchinson family, among existing evergreens and the use of foundation plantings served to minimize its impact on the landscape.
OUR COUNTRY HOME, 1908

can walk in, and live in, and not merely admire as it hangs on the wall. If the picture is beautiful, it is well done, though all the traditions and conventions . . . may be violated. And if the picture is not beautiful and interesting, then it is poorly done, though it may conform to all the conventions, as many dull gardens do.[29]

Wisconsin Horticulture readers enthusiastically embraced the idea of individuality in the garden, as can be seen in the numerous articles and reports by members. One of particular interest details the 1930 member outing to Wychwood, the Lake Geneva summer estate of the Chicago-based Hutchinson family. In marked contrast to the formality of the Mitchell estate, Wychwood had been carefully designed to retain the native vegetation of the site and protect the lakeshore. With its low elevation, overhanging roof, horizontal lines, and half-timbered Tudor-style elements, the house was supposedly reminiscent of William Shakespeare's home in Stratford-upon-Avon in England. In the photo accompanying the article, the outline of the house, which was tucked into the surrounding wooded areas, is blurred with vine-covered porches and pergolas. Winding pathways edged in local stone led to hidden garages and rustic outbuildings. The estate's many gardens were designed by an unnamed landscape architect working closely with

Frances Kinsley Hutchinson and contained a wealth of native plants and shrubs described in detail in her book about the building of the home and garden.[30]

The contrast between the Hutchinson and Mitchell estates is an indication of the changes that occurred both in architectural and landscape ideals and fashions over sixty years. The Mitchell house stood isolated, solid, and massive within its grounds, symbolizing prosperity and success. Its ornate iron fence, signifying the boundary of the estate, enclosed formal gardens that could be viewed both by the family from the safety of the interior of the home and by passersby on the street or sidewalk. On the other hand, Wychwood was intended to interact with the landscape and almost disappear into the surrounding woods and water. The organic connection between the house and grounds was emphasized by the use of foundation plantings, vines, curved border plantings, pergolas, and native species. The many enclosed gardens were outdoor rooms for the family, who used them for eating, working, gardening, and entertaining. According to Frances Kinsley Hutchinson, she and her husband continued to add gardens, beds, plants, and even outbuildings to the original design, making it a constantly changing landscape. Although they, like the Mitchells, relied on a full-time gardener, they had a much more interactive and personal relationship with their garden.

The estates can hardly be more dissimilar, yet each epitomized the latest gardening styles of the time. Neither estate would be considered vernacular: both homes were architecturally designed in the fashion of the period, as were their gardens, for wealthy community leaders. However, the fact that they were included in WSHS publications indicates that their designs were relevant to their particular time period and could serve as actual models for the average Wisconsin gardener.

By 1930 the interaction of people and the garden was acknowledged: people should *live in* the garden rather than simply admire it. This, in part, explains the contrast between the appearance and composition of the Mitchell and Hutchinson estates and the changes in the vernacular garden throughout the state. The WSHS presentations traced the evolution of the Wisconsin home garden and, in their published form, proved valuable guides to those looking for ideas on beautifying their surroundings.

Beautifying the Home Grounds

Among the external means for creating such an attractiveness to our homes, we think none so universally available, and which will yield more abundant rewards, than a well planned and thoroughly and neatly cultivated flower garden. It is surprising what stores of domestic, social and moral wealth such a plat of ground will yield; what rewards of refined pleasure, of elevation of morals; what cultivation of higher instincts and purer tastes; what stimulants to thought, to domestic love, to disrelish the fallacies and intoxications of an impetuous and feverish society; what elements and fields of rest to the weary, of consolation to the desponding, of wealth to the poor.

DR. H. ALLEN, 1880[1]

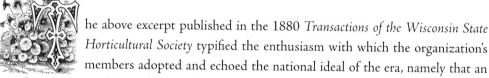he above excerpt published in the 1880 *Transactions of the Wisconsin State Horticultural Society* typified the enthusiasm with which the organization's members adopted and echoed the national ideal of the era, namely that an "impetuous and feverish society" would benefit from a closer relationship with nature. This concept continued to be a guiding force underlying the changes that occurred in garden design in the early twentieth century.

For the most part, Wisconsinites followed the national trends in the appearance and function of their gardens. Geometric carpet beds with their vivid colors and intricately designed textures and patterns gave way to looser, softer, and more naturalistic flowing border plantings. Harsh magentas and intense purples were replaced with

This vintage hand-colored photograph shows a section of the Kneeland-Walker House cutting garden in Wauwatosa as it looked circa 1920. Though this particular garden is no longer extant, other parts of the garden retain their vintage form and are interpreted by house staff. COURTESY OF WAUWATOSA HISTORICAL SOCIETY

delicate pastels that drifted and billowed against the exterior of the house. Outdoor rooms for family use intersected with sleeping porches, verandas, and patios to create an organic relationship between the home and its immediate surroundings.

The "improvement," "beautification," or "ornamentation" of home grounds was a frequent topic at WSHS meetings from 1869 to 1930. Almost three hundred papers on the subject were published, either in *Transactions of the Wisconsin State Horticultural Society*, the *Annual Reports*, *The Wisconsin Horticulturist*, or *Wisconsin Horticulture*. Of these, thirty-one specifically addressed the layout of home grounds, while several others included this subject within their main topic.[2]

Probably because of Wisconsin's population distribution, the WSHS placed more emphasis on planning and planting rural home grounds than did national publications, at least until the turn of the twentieth century. Increased attention to the design of the urban landscape after 1900 was likely a result of the changing demographic distribution within the state, as the agricultural workforce relocated to manufacturing jobs in urban areas. However, the rural home landscape continued to interest WSHS writers well into the 1930s.

The definitive recommendations for layout and composition of the Wisconsin garden was the 1904 article "The Improvement of Home Grounds," written by Frederic Cranefield and published both as *Bulletin 105* of the Wisconsin Agricultural Experiment Station and appended to the WSHS *Annual Report*.[3] This article, which summarized the contemporary landscape recommendations of the day and provided practical plans for implementation, was based not only on Cranefield's own expertise but also on the acknowledged influence of nationally respected landscape professionals Liberty Hyde Bailey and Warren H. Manning. To strengthen his arguments, Cranefield included diagrammatic landscape plans for unimproved and improved rural, suburban, and village lots, as well as photographs of rural and urban homes. His article provides documentary and pictorial evidence for the appearance of Wisconsin vernacular home grounds during this period and appears to have been adopted as the standard for WSHS recommendations, since few subsequent presentations of the topic appeared until after Cranefield left his post as the society's secretary in 1926.[4] Its professional approach also signified the change that Cranefield and others were attempting to initiate within the WSHS to make it a more academic and professional organization.

The majority of presentations followed a similar pattern that included subtopics pertaining to five broad themes: home and outbuilding placement and differentiation of space into public, private, and work areas; boundary and fencing elements; appearance of lawn, paths, and driveways; placement of trees, shrubs, flower beds, small fruit and vegetable gardens, and various specialty gardens; and the use of native plants in the home grounds. Each subtopic was well represented by many different speakers throughout the six decades covered in this book. Early speakers tended to repeat the recommendations of national garden publications, but, as will be discussed later in this chapter, the emergence of a regional consciousness can be traced through these presentations, as WSHS members gradually began to address the particular requirements of the Wisconsin homeowner.

Building Placement and Differentiation of Space

By 1870 the idea of differentiating the home grounds into public, work, and private family areas had been addressed by many nationally known landscape professionals. Andrew Jackson Downing, Jacob Weidenmann, and others had suggested that the area in front of the suburban or urban residence should be open to public view, while work areas behind the house containing the stable or barn, outbuildings, drying lawn or laundry area, and the kitchen garden should be secluded from public sight with fencing or shrubbery.

Downing and others had also made suggestions for the architectural style of the residence and its placement on the lot. In Wisconsin these rules had already been interpreted and presented by Milwaukee nurseryman Thomas Hislop, a speaker at the 1852 Wisconsin State Agricultural Society annual meeting and a founding member of the WSHS. After suggesting the location and orientation of the rural home that would provide the best use of shade, sun, and shelter, Hislop pondered the most suitable style for the house, stating that a square or oblong residence had the least availability of "aspect"—meaning views from the windows—but that the Gothic style recommended by Downing may not have been the best fit for the Wisconsin prairie, in spite of the irregularity that allowed "a variety of aspects" from various windows:

> The spirit of the Gothic style, more than any other, admits of this irregularity; and hence, the prevalence of that style in modern country residences. Among the advantages of this irregular style, one is that it readily admits of additions in almost any direction, without compromising the character of the tout ensemble. When, however, a rigid adherence to the principles of good taste is aimed at, this style may not be always in keeping with the character of the neighboring grounds or surrounding country. Perhaps the more regular style of the Roman, or the simple style of the Grecian, would be more in place.[5]

In his recommendation that the farm outbuildings be placed a distance from the house and concealed with walls or vegetation, Hislop applied the rules of space allocation also recommended by Downing. Private recreational space was not considered necessary on the rural farm; in fact, even in 1900 open vistas were considered an antidote to rural isolation, as noted by Charles Ramsdell, a Menomonie horticulturist who was a spokesperson for Warren H. Manning:

> Here of course no seclusion is necessary. In fact, most people in the country wish to see all that is going on and rightly so, for their life is at best an isolated one. Therefore no family lawn or outdoor parlor if you so choose to call it, is needed. A level lawn or meadow in front of the house with barn and outbuildings at the back or side as much out of sight as possible, is the simplest arrangement.[6]

H. W. S. Cleveland discussed the placement of the rural home in extensive detail in his 1873 *Landscape Architecture, As Applied to the Wants of the West*, recommending that the residence be located below the summit of the land rather than at its crest, which would give it a "bleak, exposed look."[7] The house could then serve as a screen to hide the working areas from public view. He went on to describe in detail how to place outbuildings, roads, and paths for ease of access, convenience, and privacy.[8]

Early WSHS guidelines for home placement and differentiation of space included the following excerpt from a presentation at the 1885 annual meeting:

> *Begin by placing the dwelling house eight or ten rods* [132 to 166 feet] *from the highway, with the barn still further back, and a little to one side, rather than across the road in front of the parlor windows. The vegetable and fruit gardens should be in the rear of the house and near the kitchen and barn.*[9]

Emmet S. Goff, the director of the Department of Horticulture at the University of Wisconsin, gave one of the first professional papers on landscape architecture at the 1890 WSHS meeting. In "The Adornment of Home Grounds" he mainly addressed the placement of trees and shrubs but also brought the concept of a larger-scale view into the layout of the home landscape:

> *Very few home grounds are so beautiful in themselves that the outlooks from the dwelling may not be rendered more attractive by including within the view pleasing objects from beyond the grounds. We should seek to plant in such a way that our own trees and shrubs may form part of a landscape that is not limited to the area immediately surrounding the house, but stretches far away to pleasing objects in the distance.*[10]

In 1900 *The Wisconsin Horticulturist* recommended Warren H. Manning's *A Handbook for Planning and Planting Small Home Grounds* to its subscribers.[11] Publicity in Wisconsin for the Manning pamphlet, through the WSHS and in *The Wisconsin Horticulturist*, probably added to its regional significance. Manning's guidelines for differentiation of space are important because they were adopted by Cranefield in his influential 1904 article. The following excerpt defines the prevailing thought on the differentiation of space for small home grounds—both urban and rural—including the concepts of connecting lawns between houses and making outdoor rooms easily accessed from the indoors:

Ordinarily the principal subdivisions of a small space would be, first, an entrance section or front lawn; second, a living section or back lawn, and third, a service or work area.

The first would be the lawn space between the front of the house and street which is so often made continuous by the removal of front and side fences. If front fences are maintained, a border plantation may be made directly back of them to give the desired seclusion to the home grounds, and both front and back lawns may thus be thrown together. If fences are removed, then this semi-public front lawn should have nearly continuous groups of planting at the base of each house, and from house to house, to screen persons on the piazzas and back lawns from the gaze of strangers in the street. Such plantations should not, however, break the continuity of this lawn area next to the street.

The second would be the lawn area at the side and back of the house which will be enclosed by the groups of shrubbery between it and the front lawn and the adjoining properties. This area should be so conveniently arranged and so readily accessible from the living rooms of the house that it will be used as freely during pleasant weather as are the living rooms. It may be a simple open turf, framed in by the screening and border plantations, or it may be subdivided into a flower-garden, terrace, game courts, etc., as space and means will allow.

The third or working section, which should be screened from the other parts by vine-covered fences, hedges, or belts of shrubs, and entered from the street by an independent walk or road, would embrace the kitchen yard, the kitchen garden, the laundry yard, and the stable and its yards, all so arranged as to be readily accessible from each other and from the kitchen and cellar.[12]

Manning continued with recommendations for plantings that would screen and separate different areas, "uniting buildings with grounds by a clothing of vines, and by planting around foundations, etc." This is an early reference to the use of foundation plantings, a garden fashion that would be universally adopted in the ensuing few years.

Charles Ramsdell, who was obviously familiar with Manning's plan, reiterated the main points at the 1900 WSHS summer meeting in Wausau, adding the suggestion that the side lawn be used as "a sort of outdoor parlor . . . divided from the front or public lawn by shrubs or lattices."[13] Ramsdell's WSHS article was one of the first to specifically address the needs of the urban homeowner, including advice on the best location of the house to afford both easy accessibility from the street and relief from street dust and noise while still allowing reasonably sized front, back, and side lawns.

This well-dressed couple appears to be enjoying their lovely garden, photographed by Andreas Larsen Dahl circa 1873. Separated from the house by a narrow lawn, the rectangular beds are bordered by straight pathways and contain a mix of very healthy annual and perennial flowers, including tall snapdragons. Trellised vines and small orchard trees form the boundary of the garden beds, with vines also climbing the porch supports.

WHI IMAGE ID 27008

Mature trees are planted inside this interesting fence, circa 1874. The landscaping inside the fence is unusually well planned, although the grass is obviously scythed rather than mowed.
The buggy inside the fence is thought to belong to Dahl.

WHI IMAGE ID 26452

A simple wooden fence encloses a lawn that contains poplar and pine trees, circa 1873. Interestingly, the annual vines, probably morning glories, have been trained to cover the windows completely—possibly to cool and darken interior rooms during the hot summer months.

WHI IMAGE ID 26978

This unknown group, circa 1873, is playing croquet in front of a picket fence that encloses a shady yard and several well-established mature trees. Notice the trellis at the side of the house and the shrubs in front of the porch.

WHI IMAGE ID 27458

As Wisconsin's towns and villages grew, WSHS speakers continued to discuss and recommend appropriate placement for a home site, while sometimes editorializing on the building practices of their growing communities. F. C. Edwards offered an interesting firsthand observation of the lack of building planning in 1901, an explanation for the resulting problems, and his recommendations for future development:

I am sorry to say that a large percentage of our people in the cities and towns have their houses six to fifteen feet from the street walk or avenue, and this being the case we have no lawn to decorate in a satisfactory manner. This fault is largely due to the fact that one neighbor crowds to the walk and the next builder, in order not to be shut in, does likewise, till all the builders in the street have followed the example of the first offender. No dwelling house should be closer than 40 to 60 feet from the street walk in front, and this would guarantee opportunity to grow or have shade and ornamental trees in the frontage and on the side and backgrounds. There is space enough in this world to have all lots not less than 4 rods wide and 8 rods deep [66 by 132 feet], and if possible these dimensions should be doubled. This question of room is crowding the best builders into the suburbs, on the lake fronts and into the country. The farmer has by far the best chance to have and own a beautiful lawn and drives.[14]

In his 1903 presentation "Home Grounds," Caldwell resident Delbert Utter underscored Edwards's argument for country living, stating that farm homes were "the great strength of this republic" and, moreover, that "the influence of city life is demoralizing and unmakes the natural man." Utter recommended the following boundaries for rural sites:

When we speak of home grounds we do not mean the front yard but the back yard as well, the barnyard, the garden, the adjoining fields and the roadside. . . . The out-buildings should be in the back ground, making the house the center and most prominent part. . . . [Frame the house] using trees and shrubbery for the frame and also fences if you wish. . . . If the house is of stone or one of those low rambling kind, let the grounds follow nature's lines . . . while if the house is of a stiff modern type, then let the lines be more formal.[15]

The Dahl photographs here and on pages 31–36 illustrate the differing placement of homes on the city or rural lot that Edwards and Utter wrote about. Generally, rural homes were set back with a large front yard, while city homes tended to be placed closer to the street.

Cranefield's landmark 1904 article was the first to include plans for the layout of home grounds. While his text did not specify guidelines for placement of the home and differentiation of space within the grounds, the diagrams, which show original and improved plans for rural, suburban, and village homes, clearly indicated his recommendations. (The origin of these plans is unclear. Some sketches in the same article are reproduced from Bailey's *Garden-making*, originally published in 1898, although they are not specifically referenced. Possibly these are Cranefield's own designs.)

The original plan shows a rural home with a short, straight path leading from the highway to the house and a long driveway along the length of the property behind the home providing access to outbuildings. Intersecting highways form the property boundaries. Six large trees in a roughly quincunx pattern to the left of the home are the only horticultural elements. Cranefield's improvements called for the removal of these large trees to create a more open area of lawn, a repositioning of the working driveway for shorter and easier access to the highway, and extensive use of trees and shrubs for clearer boundary definition. Curving borders and edging patterns; screening of what is presumably the outhouse; and defined areas of lawn, separated by the paths and screens, are additional landscape elements. Significantly, Cranefield added foundation plantings around the front of the house, resulting in a softening of the rectangular appearance of the lot without the loss of boundary definition. This example illustrates that the differentiation of space into private and public areas was not considered important for rural homes.

Cranefield's original suburban home layout consisted of a pathway to the house lined with shrubs, a star-shaped carpet bed on the front lawn surrounded by several trees that probably interfered with the view to and from the house itself, and very little "improvement," meaning landscaping, in other areas. Cranefield repositioned and curved the entry path to allow a larger open area of lawn in the front of the house, removed the carpet bedding and trees from the same area, and again screened the outhouse with shrubs. The rectangles outlined by dotted lines on the plan probably indicate a vegetable garden and an orchard. Again, foundation plantings were recommended around the front and sides of the house, and lot boundaries were defined with trees and shrubs.

Frederic Cranefield's suggestions for the improvement of a rural landscape. The image at left depicts the original landscape; at right are his suggested changes.

ANNUAL REPORT OF THE WISCONSIN STATE HORTICULTURAL SOCIETY, 1904

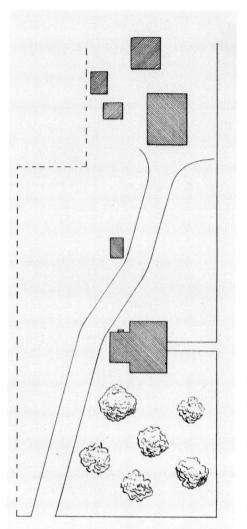

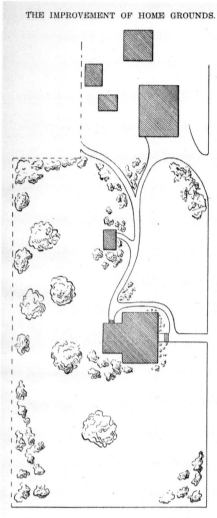

THE IMPROVEMENT OF HOME GROUNDS.

FIG. 11.—Improvements suggested for Fig. 10.

In this instance, however, the differentiation of space into public and private areas was defined by the use of vegetation.

In Cranefield's recommendation for improving a village lot, he defined the boundaries with corner plantings and created two private areas—one directly behind the house and one to the left of the driveway—by incorporating plant screenings. He removed trees that screened the front of the house from the street, and, rather than foundation plantings, he added corner elements to soften the edges of the house.

Further documentation on the layout of home grounds did not appear in WSHS literature until ten years later, when Oconomowoc landscape architect E. H. Niles published a landscape plan to accompany his article, "Planting the Home Grounds," in the February 1914 issue of *Wisconsin Horticulture*.[16] Not surprisingly, the plan was for a rural farm—it would be 1930 before an urban lot design appeared within the WSHS literature—and included many of the elements Cranefield discussed in 1904, providing evidence that Cranefield's plan was not only valid but also functional over time. Niles explained the design in detail; this excerpt offers a valuable example of the rationale for the layout of a 1914 farm garden:

> *The trees in rows on each side of the house are fruit trees and they are filled in between with berrybushes and vegetables. The stars in the back of the lawn are Evergreens and make a background for the lawn as well as a screen for the barn. The Plum trees are*

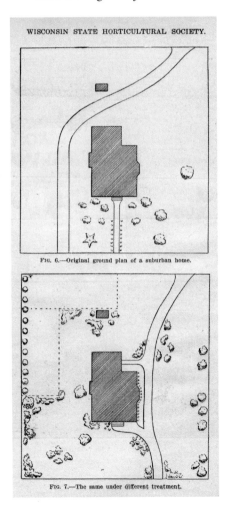

Left: Cranefield's improvements for a suburban garden
ANNUAL REPORT, 1904

Right: Cranefield's recommendations for improving a village lot
ANNUAL REPORT, 1904

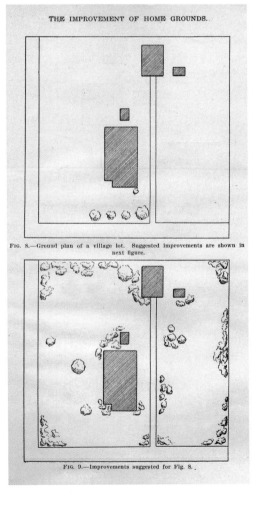

E. H. Niles's landscape
plan for a rural home in
Oconomowoc

WISCONSIN HORTICULTURE,
FEBRUARY 1914

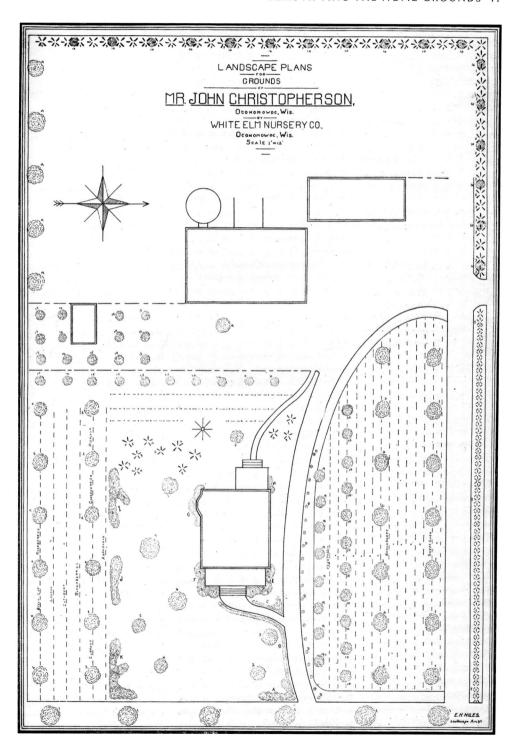

placed in the chicken yard as that is probably the best place. The first row to the south of
the lawn is Asparagus and the beds along the edge and near the house are shrubs and
flowers. This gives a nice open lawn bordered with shrubs and flowers and an abundance
of fruit all on a compact piece of land that will not be difficult to take care of.[17]

In Niles's plan the organization of space within the home grounds is geometric, but asymmetric, as was typical of this time period. The strongly geometric boundaries of the home grounds are emphasized by the use of evergreens to demarcate the lot dimensions. The house outlines are softened by foundation plantings while curved driveways ease the otherwise strong geometric lines of the lot.

The next presentation to specifically address the layout of home grounds was that of C. E. Carey, a professor of landscape gardening at the University of Minnesota, who delivered a talk on the subject at the 1925 WSHS annual meeting in Eau Claire. Carey's presentation included theories of landscape architecture such as the importance of form, texture, and color; the need for harmony between home and garden; and the importance of a proper plan. In the following passage his emphasis on the input of a landscape architect indicates how far the profession had come:

Having selected the site for our home . . . we are presented with the problem of placing
this house and its architectural accompaniments so that it may appear as one with
the site, as it belonged there and nowhere else, the first step toward unity in our
picture. . . . [O]nce our buildings are located, the size and shape of the remaining
areas are determined . . .

  There is, or should be, such a close relationship between the rooms inside the
house and the out-of-door rooms. The ideal is met when the house designer, home
owner, and landscape architect work hand in hand from the beginning.[18]

This was followed in 1928 by a series of articles in *Wisconsin Horticulture* that underlined the importance of proper site location and planning. Landscape architect E. A. Petranek reiterated many of Cranefield's recommendations in "It's Not a Home Until It's Planted," his three-part essay that addressed the careful placement of corner elements such as small trees and shrubs, the use of foundation plantings, and the separation of public and private spaces.[19]

It appears that professional input was by this time considered a necessity—at least according to the landscape architect. This is clearly indicated in "Design in the Garden," an article in the March 1930 issue of *Wisconsin Horticulture*. The unidentified writer

Above: Recommendations for the home garden, as illustrated in the March 1930 *Wisconsin Horticulture* article "Design in the Garden"

Right: Alfred L. Boerner's plan for an English-style garden
WISCONSIN HORTICULTURE, MARCH 1930

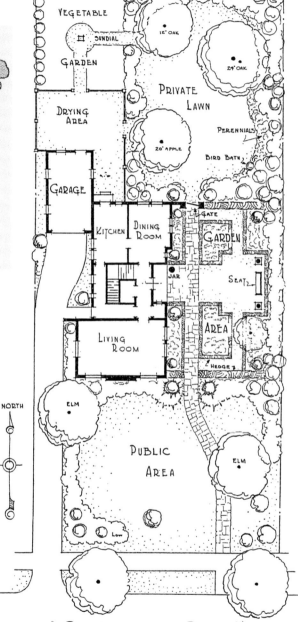

A DEVELOPMENT PLAN FOR
· LANDSCAPING OF AN ENGLISH HOME
THE BOERNER Co
LANDSCAPE ARCHITECTS·

emphasized the importance of such design principles as the central axis point of the garden and elements of composition, and concluded by stating that "[g]arden design is difficult to explain, and perhaps not easy for a novice to understand."[20] In the sketch that accompanied the article (previous page, left), the rules of differentiation of space into public and private areas were essentially the same as those defined by Scott and Weidenmann sixty years previously: note the strong geometric though asymmetric components of the design, heavy foundation and boundary planting, and the long driveway with a turnaround that now led to a garage rather than a barn. The two figures overseeing the plan appear to be landscape architects, implying the need for professional insight to interpret and implement the rules correctly—this despite the assertion by the same author that old gardening traditions no longer needed to be followed.[21]

This plan is also of interest for the fact that it closely resembles the landscape plan for an "English-type house" designed by landscape architect Alfred L. Boerner and published in *Wisconsin Horticulture* in the same year. The English-style elements of the design are seen in the hedged side garden that incorporates raised geometric flower beds and the small lawn edged by a long terrace. This type of enclosed "garden room" was popularized by Gertrude Jekyll and others in England around the turn of the twentieth century.[22]

Although these examples show landscapes that were professionally designed, they do have relevance for the vernacular garden because they were published in *Wisconsin Horticulture* and disseminated to the WSHS membership. Owners of vernacular gardens could then adapt the original design, in much the same way they adapted architecturally designed houses, to accommodate their particular budget, taste, and interests.

Boundary and Fencing Elements

The WSHS literature and recommendations for the delineation of boundaries and edges generally followed national trends. The geometric boundaries of both rural and urban home grounds are unmistakably laid out on the landscape, usually in the form of a square or rectangle, following the section and range division of the land.

WSHS speakers recommended that the boundaries of the rural home grounds be strongly defined with trees, shrubs, or fences so as to separate them from the surrounding fields and protect them from wandering animals; this recommendation did not change between 1869 and 1930. There were, however, differing opinions on how to define the boundaries of farm home grounds.

As early as 1852, Thomas Hislop, speaking at the Wisconsin State Agricultural Society meeting, had noted that fencing was a considerable expense for the average farmer and, therefore, "it would be well for settlers thereon to provide themselves at the outset, with

Example of "A Neat Farm Home," showing trees and a painted fence. The original caption read: "Everything about this farm home indicates prosperity and what is of more importance, a regard for appearances. A lawn mower is here considered a necessity rather than a luxury. . . . Some of the niceties of landscape art may have been overlooked but the right spirit is shown. At least this much is due from each of us to the community in which we live."

WISCONSIN HORTICULTURE,
APRIL 1915

seeds of such plants or shrubs as will most rapidly or permanently afford them live fences or hedges. Of these may be mentioned the Osage Orange, Locust, Buckthorn, Hawthorn, Beech, etc."[23]

Hislop particularly recommended the Osage Orange, which he said would form a thick, compact, cattle-proof barrier within five years. He disliked the look of the "common rail or zig-zag," calling it uncouth and a waste of timber. "The improved state of the manufacture of fence iron affords new and desirable accommodations in the way of light, cheap and durable fences, desiderata of no small importance in districts where wood is not abundant," he noted.[24] The Dahl photographs (pages 31–36) offer evidence of the wide variety of fencing and boundary materials and design during the 1870s.

An 1898 article in *The Wisconsin Horticulturist* strongly recommended installation of a "Page Fence" to delineate the boundaries of farm homes. This fifty-eight-inch wire fence was described as ornamental enough for any farm and was even suggested as a way to keep "the boys and girls" on the farm, since it created a sense of neatness and order.[25] In his 1904 article Cranefield appeared to disagree with this solution:

Boundaries of farm homes should be sharply defined so that there may be no doubt where the lawn ends and the fields begin. Groups or banks of trees and shrubs serve admirably for this purpose. If the border line exceeds one hundred feet in length good effect may be had by planting in irregular outline with bays and recesses but such irregularities of outline on small places are rarely as effective as a straight line . . .

Substantial fences should separate the lawn from adjoining fields, as well as from the barnyards, but there is an increasing tendency, at least in the older settled portions of the state, to dispense with the fence in front of the house, and generally with marked improvement. A fence is never an ornamental feature in a landscape.[26]

Nevertheless, in the same article Cranefield stated that isolated homes should be surrounded with a substantial fence, preferably wire, and that they should include an automatic closing device.[27]

Photographs of farms in *Wisconsin Horticulture* during the first decades of the twentieth century show that trees, hedges, or split-rail fences were often chosen to define rural lot boundaries.

Urban and suburban dwellings were located on geometrically shaped lots that already had strong boundary elements, usually composed of some type of fencing. The iron fencing mentioned by Hislop in 1852 seems to have been a popular choice for enclosing the front lawn of the urban or village home during the late nineteenth century. Mrs. Vie Campbell, a frequent speaker at WSHS meetings, preferred "various wire and decorative iron fences" to the traditional picket fence. Board fences, she said, should not be built too high as they restrict the view of the passerby. If a hedge was the choice for boundary delineation, she argued it should be kept well trimmed.[28] Hedges of "hardy roses, such as have lived for a century in eastern gardens, or the old time lilacs with their sweet bloom, or the honeysuckle, or the snowball, will always give pleasure," noted Mrs. D. Huntley.[29]

F. C. Edwards, speaking in 1901, also suggested a shrub boundary or, failing that, vines to soften a fence:

Every lawn has a divide from the adjoining one by fence, evergreen or shrub hedge. If a fence, vines can be used with good effect as a partial cover, such as honeysuckles, trumpet vines, bitter sweet and some sorts of ivy. I very much prefer a shrub hedge, and if you want a low border, spirea Thunbergii is excellent. If a higher hedge spirea Van Houteii or barberry. Vines can be made a great attraction on the porches, pillars or corners.[30]

Another option was the rustic fence, described by Mrs. D. Huntley of Appleton, "made of wide rough pickets driven into the ground a few inches apart and, woven together at the top with willows."[31] But in 1895 A. L. Hatch promoted the advantages of fence removal:

When you go through the streets of a city you see a long line of wall or a fence, and it looks as if you were shut out; it does not look as if you were welcome. Now let us lend our influence as a Society to bring about a change, and instead of fenced streets bordered with unsightly weeds and a place to pile up the brush and old rubbish, let us have nice, well-kept boulevards and shady streets bordered with grass.[32]

As early as 1870, Weidenmann and Cleveland were advocating the removal of fencing between adjoining houses and between the street and the house. In 1873, they highly recommended an unbroken stretch of lawn along a city block, stating that fences and gates along city streets were usually unmatched and therefore ugly.[33] However, it appears that it was not until the 1890s that this concept was addressed by WSHS speakers. At the 1902 meeting, F. E. Pease discussed the cultural differences of the English and Americans in terms of lot boundaries and recommended a compromise between the extremes of complete enclosure or none at all:

The English idea is to exclude the public gaze altogether by a wall of some kind. The American idea seems to be to throw the grounds wide open to public view. In my opinion, a medium between those extremes is best. I like to have the grounds enclosed in some manner. There is then a sense of ownership and privacy not afforded by unenclosed areas. My preference for a street line enclosure is a brick or stone base wall surmounted by a neat iron fence. The wall and fence at path and drive entrances to curve . . . and terminate at good substantial gate pillars. . . . The side lines may be enclosed with any neat fence or hedge.[34]

Discussion of the fashion of removing front fences was even mentioned by Wisconsin writer Zona Gale. In *Birth*, the 1918 novel based on her life in Portage, she observed:

City water was acquired, and on Summer evenings you no longer heard the rhythmic sweep of a whetstone sharpening a blade. . . . Lawns became green and tended. Here and there remained a wire fence whose owner resisted the nagging advances of the women of his household, seeking to have the fence removed "like other folks": but fences in general had remained for fifteen years after cattle had ceased to roam the highways. Nor is that genius memorialized who at last arose and challenged the reason for fences, and boldly took down his own.[35]

This example of a lattice fence, sent in by a WSHS member, was accompanied by instructions on its construction.

WISCONSIN HORTICULTURE, SEPTEMBER 1915

Why Not Build One Like This?

Boundary elements for urban home grounds apparently continued to be a decision of personal choice, possibly influenced by prevailing neighborhood or civic improvement ideals that called for unified street landscapes. However, beginning in about 1890, there is a change in the type of material recommended for boundary elements, with vegetation—especially the use of hardy shrubs—replacing wood or iron fencing to define the perimeter and internal differentiation of home grounds. The lattice fence was also a popular choice because its attractive open structure also served as vine support.[36]

The move from precise geometric boundaries toward a more natural flow and a softening of boundary elements is expressed in this excerpt from a presentation at the 1925 WSHS annual meeting that echoed the recommendations of landscape architects like Grace Tabor and Fletcher Steele:

> [W]alls there must be if we are to secure the privacy necessary to the fullest use and enjoyment of our rooms. Walls of earth, of masonry, of frame or of plant forms— the severely trimmed hedge, the informal shrub border, the vine clad wall or fence. And as in our house walls we find various openings for various purposes, so out-of-doors the walls surrounding or dividing our out-door rooms will be broken here and there with doors, enabling us to circulate freely for maintenance and pleasure,— and with windows opening out to an attractive view of permitting the sun's rays to aid the growth of some choice group of flowers.[37]

By the 1920s, according to the WSHS literature, the prevailing view was that boundaries should be de-emphasized, softened, and blurred with shrubs or vines, while street and interconnecting fencing between homes should be removed.

Appearance of Lawn, Paths, and Driveways

Between 1869 and 1930 WSHS speakers and authors agreed that the lawn should be as large and unbroken as possible, that it should be a greensward that extended from the front of the residence to the boundary of the home grounds, and that it should be framed with clumps of trees, shrubs, or flower beds—the main principles that earlier landscape professionals like Downing had laid down for the outline of the lawn. Cranefield noted: "It is an axiom in landscape art that the largest possible space of lawn should be maintained open and free. This gives the impression of breadth and extent which is always desirable."[38] As lawn mowers became more universally available, this look was easier to maintain. Tree planting on the lawn was frowned upon, although some writers accepted the presence of a few specimen trees on the lawn as long as they did not interfere with the view to or from the home itself.

Before and after diagrams, illustrating Cranefield's ideas on the correct way to plant a front lawn. *ANNUAL REPORT*, 1904

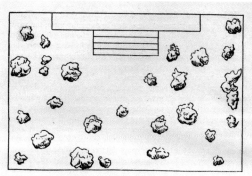

FIG. 2.—Planted but not planned.

FIG. 3.—"A definite plan has been followed."

However, even with these principles in place, a marked change occurred in the appearance of the lawn. During the mid-1800s the prevailing national fervor had been to cut complex shapes in the lawn and fill them with vibrant annual plants to mimic Oriental rugs, and according to an essay Mrs. Laura Smith wrote for the Wisconsin State Agricultural Society in 1853, this fashion had reached Wisconsin by that time:

Flower beds are now frequently cut in circles and various other forms in the turf, using the turf itself as a walk; this is very beautiful in extensive grounds, or even in a small grass plat. The usual manner, however, is to form beds in various pleasing figures—leaving wide walks between the principal beds. For full directions I will refer my lady readers to "Breck's Book of Flowers," which no one should fail to consult when arranging a flower garden.[39]

Although this type of bed was recommended by most speakers until the 1880s, the problems associated with its maintenance were acknowledged:

If one has a large lawn, a few beds cut in it can be made very effective; but to have this, the lawn-mower must be kept often in use, for the pleasing effect would be lost if the grass were allowed to grow too tall.[40]

Speakers recommended bedding plants such as verbena, pansies, and geraniums— grown from seed in hotbeds or in an indoor window—for mass planting. Many suggested that a bulb bed full of tulips or other bulbs should be planted toward the front of the lawn near the road and that annuals could later fill this bed.

View of Wisconsin farm home. Cranefield's original caption read: "The lawn has been preserved, and this with the large tree almost provides a restful picture. A group of trees to the left would screen the outhouse and define the boundary of the lawn."
ANNUAL REPORT, 1904

Example of a farm home that needed improvements. Cranefield noted: "The house would scarcely attract attention without the vine. If the tree and shrub at the left were both removed the view would be greatly improved. A single large shade tree would be valuable. Shrubs and other flowering plants might then be planted near the house."
ANNUAL REPORT, 1904

Yet, in Wisconsin, as in other parts of the country, a gradual change was occurring. In 1894 Cranefield had suggested that the lawn contain various cutout beds for annuals, with shapes that would complement the walks and drives.[41] By 1904 he had reversed this opinion, saying that the lawn should be unbroken and that the right place for flowers was at the side or in the back of the house. Cranefield's reversal can be traced to "Planning and Planting Home Grounds," the 1900 presentation by Charles Ramsdell of Menomonie in which he stated that the "lawn should be as free from walks, drives, single shrubs, and showy flower beds as possible." (Ramsdell himself had been influenced by Warren H. Manning who, in 1899, had stated that there should be "the largest available central lawn space, in which there should be but few single specimens of shrubs and trees and no formal beds of flowers."[42]) These guidelines for planting—with garden plans showing flower beds to the side or back of the house—persisted throughout the 1930s.

Walks and driveways for the rural and urban home grounds were also regular topics of discussion in the WSHS papers. In general, the need for a straight walkway from the street to the house was accepted for the urban home; for rural homes, a wide driveway circling rather than crossing the greensward and continuing on to the rear outbuildings was the recommendation. The first choice of material for driveways was crushed gravel, while either gravel or mown grass was preferred for garden walks. As carriage barns were replaced by garages in the 1920s, both urban and rural driveways were straightened and, in the case of rural homes, a separate driveway to outbuildings was often added.

Placement of Trees, Shrubs, Flower and Vegetable Beds, and Specialty Gardens

Tree Placement

Most WSHS speakers agreed that rural homeowners should plant trees for shelter, shade, security, and boundary emphasis. During the early years of settlement, the usual practice was to clear-cut an entire acreage for farming purposes, leaving stumps in place to rot. The result, as one WSHS presenter commented, tended to be "an unprotected prairie, where, like a desert, even a few stunted trees, if found, are the exception and not the rule; where we too often look in vain about the residences of the oldest inhabitant for that 'leafy garniture,' through or by which we may estimate their value."[43]

While discussion about the varieties of trees continued from 1869 to 1930, the speakers were generally in agreement on their placement within the home grounds.

This Dahl photograph shows an example of heavy foliage overwhelming a Mazomanie home, circa 1873.

WHI IMAGE ID 24150

A Cranefield photograph of a rural Wisconsin front garden that he considered "overplanted." He also criticized the round bed that detracted from the open look of the lawn.

ANNUAL REPORT, 1904

Cranefield's 1904 article consolidated the prevailing guidelines, namely that an occasional large ornamental deciduous tree could add to the attraction of the home grounds as long as it was carefully placed. Rows or groups of mixed evergreen and deciduous trees could be used to define boundaries, frame the house and garden, and create windbreaks. His caution for urban home tree planting reflected the opinion that large specimens had no place on the city lot, except possibly to define a corner, but could be used to advantage along the street.[44] Plans for urban lots sometimes included one or two small ornamentals such as crab apples, flowering almonds, or the popular Kentucky coffee tree. In general, shrubs and small evergreens were recommended for city lawns and lots, with larger, ornamental deciduous trees used for street planting.

A common concern was that the house should remain visible from the road or street and not be completely overpowered by overgrown trees. In 1886 Mrs. Ida Tilson, speaking on "Home Adornment," referenced the beauty of "the grand, old trees" but disliked "a very prevalent American style, [which] crowds every tree possible into a yard, till roofs are moss-covered, rooms dark and mouldy, inhabitants rheumatic, and sometimes, a high wind ends the scene with a general crash." Tilson related that a rheumatic friend of hers was much improved by the "judicious trimming and topping of the dense mass which overshadowed her home."[45]

Cranefield described this urban garden as having "too much foliage." He suggested that vegetation should be thinned to improve the look of the house and its grounds. *ANNUAL REPORT, 1904*

Shrub Placement

Shrubs were a popular addition to both the rural and urban home grounds from 1869 onward. The preferred placement was to mass shrubs along boundaries rather than planting them in isolated spots on the lawn. In his 1904 article, Cranefield criticized the method of planting small shrubs individually and geometrically throughout the lawn area, noting that this type of arrangement was "planted but not planned" (see page 79).

An interesting development that reflected national changes is seen in the gradual recommendation for foundation plantings—that is, the planting of a border close to the foundation of the house. Andrew Jackson Downing had approved the use of shrubs in the 1850s but preferred to plant them in formal beds and along driveways.[46] Garden historian Denise Wiles Adams noted that one of the first recommendations she found for foundation planting was in an 1891 article in *Garden and Forest* in which Charles Eliot suggested connecting the house with the ground "by massing shrubs along the bases of the walls or piazzas."[47] According to Adams, this idea did not gain popularity until after World War I, but landscape gardeners Liberty Hyde Bailey and Eben Rexford, among others, had proposed the design much earlier. In 1910 Bailey wrote that "strong and bare foundations should be relieved by heavy planting. Fill the corners with snow-drifts of foliage. Plant with a free hand, as if you meant it." He added: "The corner by the steps is a perennial source of bad temper. The lawn-mower will not touch it, and the grass has to be cut with a butcher-knife. If nothing else comes to hand, let a burdock grow in it."[48]

A review of the WSHS literature indicates Wisconsin horticulturists may have been ahead of the national trend. The first mention of foundation planting at WSHS

Cranefield criticized rural homeowners who made no attempt to improve their home grounds. He labeled this photograph "Neglected opportunities" and went on to note: "It is scarcely conceivable that a man could live fifty years on one spot without planting a single tree or shrub for shade or ornament, yet such is the case here. The owner is a well-to-do farmer who has resided in this spot for nearly half a century, and all that time, the best rooms in his house have been exposed to afternoon sun."

ANNUAL REPORT, 1904

This photograph, with the caption "care and attention marks every feature of this well-kept place," accompanied the February 1915 *Wisconsin Horticulture* article "Improvement of Home Grounds" by Professor James G. Moore. Moore encouraged home beautification to add to the value as well as the aesthetics of the home.

Above right: An example of foundation planting on a city lot. Cranefield noted: "Shrubs are effective when massed close to the home."
ANNUAL REPORT, 1904

Right: An example of an urban home with, Cranefield noted, "The pleasing effect obtained by planting shrubs close to the home."
ANNUAL REPORT, 1904

meetings was by Charles Ramsdell in 1900, ten years before Bailey and nearly twenty years before the rest of the nation took notice. "The importance of planting against the base of buildings, or along blank walls to relieve the bare effect," Ramsdell stated, "is often overlooked."[49] Again influenced by Manning, Ramsdell encouraged planting around the base of the house to soften its lines and stated that planting around the base and sides of the house framed both the house and its front lawn. In his 1899 *A Handbook for Planning and Planting Small Home Grounds*, Manning had noted that shrub plantations could unite buildings with the grounds and cover foundations. At the 1902 WSHS meeting, F. E. Pease supported this idea, suggesting that shrubs and plantings not cover the entire house or foundations but soften them. In 1904, by which time WSHS guidelines included the use of foundation planting, Cranefield critiqued

An example of perennial planting for foundation walls
AMATEUR GARDENCRAFT, 1912

the front of a farmhouse in one of his photographs, saying that the foundations looked bare and uninviting. Other photographs from the time period confirm that foundation planting was becoming popular at least in some parts of the state.

The WSHS gardening guidelines suggested a variety of low-growing deciduous and evergreen shrubs that would provide interesting year-round texture and color, but they cautioned against using too many varieties. In 1912 William G. McLean's advice for the owner of a small lot was to "just plant a few native shrubs, up near the foundation of the house."[50] In *Amateur Gardencraft* Eben Rexford illustrated that an equally good effect could be had by planting perennials around the foundation walls.

Placement of Flower Beds and the Use of Vines

The colors, textures, and decorative aspects of flowers were considered necessities to beautify the home grounds. Between 1869 and 1900, annuals appear to have been the preferred choice because of the ease with which they could be started in hotbeds or windows—but this assumes that seeds were readily available. Native perennials could be gathered from the surrounding woods at no cost and were therefore suggested as a quick and simple way to provide an inexpensive flower garden.

In 1880 Dr. H. Allen enthusiastically recommended a very elaborate plan for a forty-foot-square flower garden to be placed within sight of the house in a sunny spot. This is an important example of a WSHS member's interpretation of parterre and carpet-bed construction for the vernacular garden. It was probably an unrealistic plan for most WSHS members because of its size, expense, and labor requirements; nevertheless, Allen's detailed description provides useful documentation of how such gardens were adapted to the Wisconsin landscape—and evidence that at least one such garden existed, since Allen indicated that the plan was based on his own garden. For landscape historians interested in reconstructing a similar period garden, the following description is invaluable:

> *Lay off a border of two and a half feet all around it for border plants, with a good wide path of at least two feet between it and the main plot, where the little olive plants may run and sport and chase each other inside the floral borders. Next make a circular bed in the centre, eight feet across, with another generous path around it.*

Now run paths from the centre bed to the border path at the centre of each side of the square, and you have left four corner beds, which you can divide by inserting in them an oval bed and some smaller squares, circulars and squares, and diamonds, having each corner a little different from the others, or the two diagonal ones similar, as your choice or your taste shall dictate. . . .

And, lastly, you may build on the north side of your plot a rustic arbor, with a tight back and open front, and seats within, facing towards your garden; and cover it with the running cypress and morning glory, and Convolvulus minor and fragrant Madeira vine. And here you may sit of a summer afternoon, with your book or needle in hand, under your own vine, inhaling the fragrance of your own flowers, and growing healthier and happier and better every moment. . . . And all this need not cost you more than five dollars.[51]

The following much simpler suggestions for beautifying the farm home, presented at the same meeting, were probably more realistic. From the tone of this talk, the speaker, Mrs. D. Huntley of Appleton, appeared to be addressing a female audience. The underlying, somewhat poignant message was that even with the never-ending work of the farmer's wife, the tiniest garden would bring happiness to her life:

Photographs of back gardens are unusual and therefore valuable for research purposes. This one shows a fence with a narrow border at its base containing a mix of plants. A board walkway has been laid along the length of the garden. A trellis divides a patio from the rest of the garden, which contains three small raised beds, some pots, and an unmowed lawn. Eben Rexford called this "making the best of circumstances." He did not say where this photograph was taken, but it is possibly in his own backyard.

FOUR SEASONS IN THE GARDEN, 1910

So, my reader . . . if you cannot have a flower garden with fanciful beds, and mounds, and pretty side walks, never grieve over it one moment; the beautiful green grass before your door is one of the finest ornaments a farm house can have; besides this, perhaps you can have a narrow bed two feet wide close to the house and all around it, in which to set your flowers, they will be very near you, where you can care for them easily. . . . But if you cannot have this, a box of earth outside the window, supported by posts or brackets, will give you quite a window garden, and you can care for that and enjoy it too. . . . If this is more than you can do, devise some way in which you can have a vine by the door, and if the soil is poor and hard, spade it deep, manure it well, add some garden soil, and in it set the dear old "morning glories." . . . [T]hen take all the rest of your flowers to the vegetable garden. Ask for a place to set verbenas and petunias near the melons and cucumbers, where the plow will not disturb them. Pansies and phlox should be set in a mass, but asters and balsams will look well in a row along the garden path.[52]

Opinions were divided on the use of annuals versus perennials, with the suggestion that room existed for both in the average garden. Carpet bedding, which relied on the intense color and season-long performance of annual plants, lost favor during the last years of the nineteenth century, although annuals continued as favorite choices for window boxes, ornamental pots, vases, and baskets. And, as always, they provided the major color in the cutting garden, although the preferred location for this garden was, by the early 1900s, behind the house, unseen by the public.

The increasing national enthusiasm for perennials can probably be traced to the rise in fashion for herbaceous borders, popularized by Alice Morse Earle in Connecticut and Gertrude Jekyll in England between 1900 and 1910. Advocates of this nostalgic or grandmother's garden introduced it into WSHS publications by the early 1900s. Typical elements included the use of informal, multitextural masses of plants of varying heights in curved borders. Wisconsin gardens of this type were well represented in photographs that appeared in *Wisconsin Horticulture* throughout the next several years, and instructions for growing and maintaining perennial flowers were the subject of numerous papers between 1869 and 1930, particularly in the early twentieth century.

Perennials were to be intermixed with shrubs along the sides of the lawn, planted in front of shrub borders, placed along the pathway leading to the front door, or in specialized cutting gardens along the side or behind the house. On the farm, the suggestion was to place perennials within the boundaries of the vegetable garden.

While the placement and type of flower beds changed between 1869 and 1930, the use of vines did not. The universal enthusiasm for "festooning" the porches and

Rexford and other garden writers of his time suggested intermixing small shrubs and perennials of differing heights and textures to create lush curved borders with season-long interest.
AMATEUR GARDENCRAFT, 1912

Above right: This modern herbaceous border at Kelton House Farm in Fredonia has been planted exclusively with heirloom varieties of perennials, herbs, and other plants, many of which date to pre-1800. Delphiniums and foxgloves add height and texture to this lovely curved bed.
COURTESY KELTON HOUSE FARM

Right: An informal border, planted with perennials of varying heights and textures along both sides of a driveway, possibly Rexford's.
FOUR SEASONS IN THE GARDEN, 1910

pillars of the home with several varieties of annual and perennial vines was a strong recommendation as well as a common practice, as illustrated in numerous photographs in *Wisconsin Horticulture* and other publications.

Vines were a quick-growing solution for porches in need of shade and for beautifying boundary fences or trellises. In many cases vines were trained up the sides of the house. Interestingly, there are no cautions about the damage that vines can cause on building

A VINE-COVERED PORCH. ONE VIRGINIA CREEPER, AMPELOPSIS ENGLEMANNI, IN FIVE YEARS ACCOMPLISHED THIS.

The rampant *Ampelopsis* recommended by Rexford is more restrained on this front porch than in the image on page 16.
WISCONSIN HORTICULTURE, JUNE 1911

material. In fact, vines were thought to provide insulation in addition to protection for the home and welcome shade. Today most landscape gardeners vehemently oppose using climbing vines against house walls due to the damage the suckers, tendrils, and leaf moisture can do to siding materials.

Native vines could easily be transplanted from the wild and numerous other vine varieties were suggested in seed catalogs and WSHS publications. Chapter 5 lists the most popular recommendations.

Vegetable Garden and Home Orchard Placement

The layout and location of vegetable or kitchen gardens were infrequent topics at early WSHS meetings. This lack of emphasis appears to substantiate James William Miller's documentation that Anglo-Americans, the membership's dominant group at the time, relied less on a wide variety of vegetables in their daily diet than did German and other northern European settlers.[53] As Miller noted, "Germans new to this country were astonished at the quantity of meat eaten by Americans, which was rounded out primarily with wheat bread and cornbread, rather than vegetables and fruit."[54] When the topic of vegetable gardens was raised, it was usually to bemoan their infrequent appearance in home grounds and the lack of fresh vegetable consumption, especially by farm families, as shown in this 1851 letter to the Wisconsin State Agricultural Society:

> *I have been led to believe, that in the Western States, generally, the importance of a Kitchen Garden, as a means of real comfort to the farmer's family, is not fully appreciated; believing, as I do, that no small importance attaches to it, not only as a matter of comfort, but also of economy.*
>
> *I think every farmer should have, at least, one acre of ground, near or adjacent to his house, that is well fenced, and kept for this purpose. This may be divided, by appropriating one portion of it to choice fruits—cherries, pears, apples, plums, and quinces. Another portion may be devoted to shrubbery, currants, raspberries, and gooseberries. And another portion to vegetables—early potatoes, sweet corn, peas, beans, onions, beets, cabbages, and asparagus, etc. Even as small a garden as one of half an acre, properly cultivated, and with a judicious selection of fruits and vegetables . . . would prove of great benefit.[55]*

In his 1869 address, WSHS President Hobbins gave specific recommendations for back gardens, but he emphasized fruits rather than vegetables:

The back garden is for use, but equally pleasant as the front. This should be laid out so as to possess a few choice fruit trees, apple, plum, crab, and if you are south enough, a pear, cherry and may be, a peach. The walks may be edged with currants, undercropped with strawberries. The fence with the south or south-west aspect should be covered with grape-vines, and that of the north with blackberries and raspberries. It is perfectly wonderful what a variety of things can be grown, both luxuries and things necessary, in a single lot of ordinary city or village size. It furnishes room for all the summer and fall vegetables, salads, etc., as well as an odd nook or spot for things purely ornamental.[56]

As time went on, the need for a vegetable or fruit garden became less pronounced, especially in the city. By the 1870s urban families had access to market vegetables, while rural homes probably used field crops such as cabbages, potatoes, and corn for home consumption. Fruit bushes and trees occasionally were included as elements of the ornamental garden but more often as a component of the vegetable garden.

An 1878 paper suggested that while farm vegetable gardens should be at least one acre in area, a square rod (272 square feet) on a village lot could provide a reasonable variety and quantity of fresh fruit.[57] Nearly fifteen years later, a paper entitled "The Kitchen Garden" given by Mrs. J. Montgomery Smith at the WSHS annual meeting in 1891 reiterated the importance of vegetables for the table, suggesting that the kitchen garden incorporate cooking herbs and flower beds, laid out in long rows, so that the "modern wheel-hoe" could be used for weeding.[58] She recommended starting seeds in a hotbed—"tomatoes, peppers, egg plant, cauliflower, broccoli, celery, okra, etc., which will be ready for transplanting to the garden, as soon as all danger of frost is over."[59] Although such an array of plants would require significant maintenance as well as space on the grounds, Wisconsin homeowners who followed this advice could satisfy their vegetable needs without going to the market.

The Wisconsin Horticulturist published papers on the layout of small village and city vegetable gardens, with the most important recommendation being that they should be as close to the house as possible for successful maintenance, including watering. In 1897 a writer described an "ideal village garden," which was located on a four-rod square tract of land adjacent to the owner's home in Omro and separated by a short walkway.[60] The garden included "wide beds for flowers" and several rows for vegetables.

Trellises—not only for peas but also for cucumbers and tomatoes—were used to save space. The author noted that this vegetable garden provided food for family and friends, and small amounts of space could be put to good use this way. *The Wisconsin Horticulturist* published "A City Garden—One Man's Experience" in September 1900. A detailed planting plan was described though not illustrated and, again, the possibility of providing fresh fruit and vegetables for one's family into January was noted.[61] This seems to have been the start of the rising interest in vegetable gardens for the city dweller, which corresponded with an increased concern about the American diet expressed in several magazines and journals and which was one of the reforms of the Progressive Era. At a discussion session after the presentation of a paper on city gardening during the 1911 summer meeting, Irving Smith asked if members would be interested in teaching urban homeowners how to grow vegetables—an idea that was received with enthusiasm:

> [I]t seems to me that we, as a horticultural society, ought . . . to give the people some idea of what can be done with . . . 25 feet square of land, or perhaps a smaller amount. If quite a number of us would take a little plot of ground and cultivate it intensively as a kitchen garden, keep an exact record of what is produced on that, to give to the city man or woman some idea of what their back yard is really worth, in pleasure as well as kitchen products, I think it would help considerably towards encouraging the work in kitchen gardens in towns. I heard for instance only a few days ago an Ashland man who has a little piece of ground in his back yard say that the amount of stuff grown on that ground supplies himself and all his neighbors around.[62]

The ensuing discussion led to the beginning of WSHS attempts to encourage city vegetable gardens, either in backyards or on empty lots. In 1912 Madison Parks Superintendent William McLean conceded that it was hard to grow vegetables, especially larger ones, on the small city lot. He announced that since vegetables needed open, airy spots "we shall endeavor to use all the vacant lots in the city for the purpose of raising vegetables."[63] These ideas eventually led to the establishment of city gardens, which were called "war gardens" at the start of American involvement in World War I but renamed "victory gardens" after 1918.

Between 1910 and 1920 there was an increase in published information about vegetable gardens. The WSHS bulletin "How to Grow Vegetables," which was distributed around the state in 1917 and appeared as several supplements in *Wisconsin Horticulture*,

❧ HOME HINTS ❧

The recipes published in *Wisconsin Horticulture* suggest that there was a significant female readership. The recipes usually consisted of few ingredients, most of which were available from the home garden, and simple preparations. Some of them introduced ingredients that are rarely seen in today's kitchens. For example, the following 1915 recipe for salsify or mock oyster—a root vegetable that was grown and eaten by European immigrants but was not as well known to people of Anglo-American descent—was adapted from a recipe sent in by a Mrs. Rorer:

> *For one dozen oyster plants, scraped, sliced and boiled until tender, drain and mash, add three eggs well beaten, salt and pepper. Drop the mixture by teaspoonfuls into a hot frying pan in which there is good, hot bacon fat, and fry to simulate fried oysters. Serve with sliced lemon.*[1]

The inclusion of this recipe and other vegetable dishes in a Wisconsin State Horticultural Society publication indicates an increased awareness of the importance of vegetables in the daily diet. While the enthusiasm for vegetable gardening appeared to wane as war memories receded and the perceived food crisis subsided, plans for vegetable gardens continued to appear sporadically in *Wisconsin Horticulture* until the late 1930s.

NOTE

1. "Salsify or Oyster Plant: Mock Oysters," *Wisconsin Horticulture* 5, no. 7 (March 1915), 112–113.

helped this cause. Members volunteered to go out into communities and teach the basics of gardening. Editorials in *Wisconsin Horticulture* documented the work that was being done by members, and for a period between 1910 and 1920 readers' recipes featuring produce from the average home garden were published.

The surprising lack of information in WSHS publications about the layout of home vegetable gardens and orchards indicates that, apart from the war years, there was little interest in how these should be planted and maintained. Given that these topics were infrequently addressed by WSHS members, it was not possible to determine if there was any significant change in recommendations for the layout of these gardens between 1869 and 1930. They were certainly not given much attention until the threat of food shortages brought vegetable gardening briefly to the forefront of horticultural discussion.

Specialty Gardens

As membership in garden and horticultural societies increased, specialty and theme-oriented home gardens became fashionable. These included herb gardens, Shakespeare gardens based on the plants mentioned in Shakespeare's plays, Elizabethan gardens, miniature gardens, and, probably the most popular given the number of *Wisconsin Horticulture* articles on the topic, rock gardens, which were sometimes called alpine gardens.

Prior to Cranefield's 1904 article, no mention of rock gardens appeared in WSHS literature, although in their own publications Bailey and Rexford both discouraged their use because of the difficulty of arranging rocks naturally. Cranefield acknowledged their presence in Wisconsin gardens but criticized their appearance, stating that although rock gardens might possibly be attractive if properly located, such as in shaded areas to the back of the garden, "when carefully constructed in the most conspicuous place on the lawn, as is generally the case, [rock gardens] become piles of rocks and nothing more."[64]

This miniature garden model, constructed of plywood, felt, and papier-mâché, graced the cover of *Wisconsin Horticulture* in January 1930. In the accompanying article, Mrs. R. H. Malisch reported on the popularity of such models as teaching tools for the principles of landscape design, and suggested that each Wisconsin garden club should build at least one model during the winter months to be exhibited at the State Flower Show later in the year.

WISCONSIN HORTICULTURE, JANUARY 1930

A 1928 example of a *Wisconsin Horticulture* reader's efforts to install a rock garden on a difficult sloping section of lawn. The photograph is interesting because it also illustrates the foundation plantings, fairly heavy vegetation around the Arts & Crafts–style house, and the young street trees in a Milwaukee neighborhood.

WISCONSIN HORTICULTURE, JULY 1928

It appears that interest in rock or alpine gardens developed after a 1924 article in *Wisconsin Horticulture* gave construction instructions. Throughout the next six years several articles appeared, as did letters from readers with descriptions and photographs of their own efforts to build rock gardens, and the use of rocks became one more element in the eclectic vernacular garden.

Use of Native Plants in the Home Grounds

The use of native plants was first suggested in the 1850s as an easy and economical way to improve the look of Wisconsin home grounds; however, throughout the following years a growing appreciation of the natural beauty, hardiness, and suitability of these trees, shrubs, and flowers led to a gradual change in the guidelines for their use. The influence of landscape gardeners and architects Warren H. Manning, Jens Jensen, O. C. Simonds, and Franz Aust no doubt had an effect on WSHS members, as did the enthusiasm of Baraboo nurseryman William Toole.

In 1852, at a WSAS meeting, Laura Smith suggested several varieties of native plants that could be transplanted from the woods—if nursery-grown perennials were unavailable or too expensive. In 1877 Mrs. D. C. Ayers of Green Bay noted, "You need not buy plants; from God's nursery in the woods, you may obtain them 'without money, and without price.'"[65] Informational talks on such topics as "Early Wild Flowers of Wisconsin"

❈ GARDEN MODELS ❈

Wisconsin garden models fit the national changes in style and fashion. The ideal for rural home grounds during this period included a large area of mown lawn, preferably unbroken, edged with curving driveways and paths; defined but softened boundaries and edges consisting of shrubs and small trees; foundation plantings along the front of the house; curved borders of perennial plants; and cutting and vegetable gardens located behind the house with the drying yard and other working buildings. The unfenced front yard was open to the street, with vine-covered porches providing the transition between outside and inside. Group plantings of shrubs defined the corners of lots. This garden model is well represented in Frederic Cranefield's 1904 sketch for rural grounds (at right) and retained its validity until 1930.

By 1900 a new model for Wisconsin urban gardens had replaced what Sharon D. Crawford referred to as the urban "Victorian" garden model. This new urban garden model closely matched national recommendations for the early-twentieth-century garden, including foundation planting around the house; large, unbroken front and back lawns with boundary elements consisting of curved flower borders; straight driveways and paths; large trees at corners; and flower beds to the side and back of the house. Vegetable gardens were included at the rear of the house. Separation of space into public and private areas continued to be expressed by the open front garden and screened back and

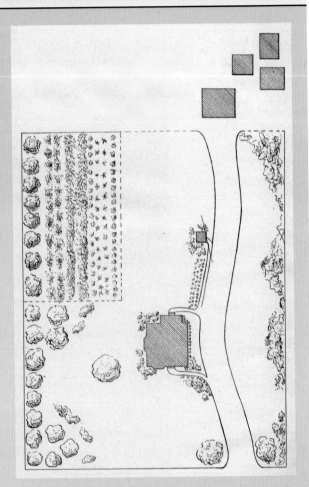

Cranefield's model for an early-twentieth-century rural garden
ANNUAL REPORT, 1904

✦ GARDEN MODELS ✦

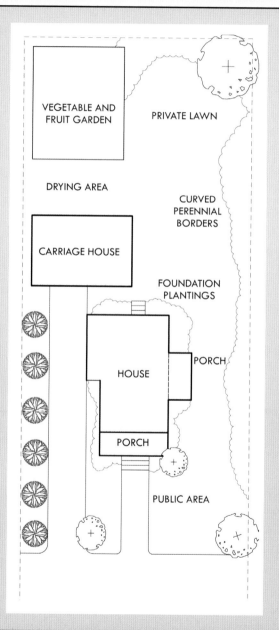

side yards. Separation of indoor and outdoor space was reduced by the use of sleeping porches, verandas, and outdoor rooms. The only major change in the model over the next two decades was the introduction of a wider driveway to the garage that eventually replaced the horse barn.

Notice the similarities between this model (at left) and May Theilgaard Watts's fourth sketch (D, page 19). Both contain a screened backyard, a porch addition, and boundary definitions created with trees and shrubs. This type of plan was certainly not unique to Wisconsin and contains many of the elements recommended in national publications.

Early-twentieth-century urban garden model
ILLUSTRATION BY DEE FINNEGAN AND LEE SOMERVILLE

(1875) and "Our Native Vines" (1877) were a fairly regular occurrence at early WSHS meetings; nevertheless, the prevailing fashion for carpet beds filled with colorful annuals resulted in the promotion of purchased nursery seeds or plants—a turn of events possibly bolstered by the high incidence of nurserymen on the membership rolls.[66] A very gradual change in the normative view of WSHS members can be traced to Professor Beal's 1885 paper, given at the Mississippi Valley Horticultural Society meeting and later reproduced in the *Transactions of the Wisconsin State Horticultural Society*. In it he made an important pronouncement:

> *Heap [a pile of stones] in some back and shady corner, and you will find great delight in transplanting from woods and meadows an assortment of hepaticas, spring beauties, blood-roots, trilliums, bell worts, phloxes and ferns. If you have a pond near by, introduce some water lilies, cat-tail, flags, pickerel weed, arrowhead, and near by set some Wisconsin weeping willows and birches and ashes. Do not despise flower, shrub or tree because it is native and "common." As a rule, the best known is better than the imported rarity.[67]*

In the same year, Mrs. Ida Tilson introduced the idea of using native plants for pleasure rather than necessity:

> *There is no more fascinating branch of flower gardening than bringing in to some shady nook or unused corner the spirit of the forest. I remember one rockery built around a deep dish for water in which grew pitcher-plants and other aquatic kinds. . . . Even a stump covered with vines and sweet white violets nestling about it, whisper of their woodland home. Wild roses, blue violets and dicentras are beauties easily domesticated. A miscellaneous bed is interesting, and a sprinkling of forest soil every autumn, will make such a one thrive for years.[68]*

Warren H. Manning's landscape plan for the Stout Manual Training School included a wide variety of native plants, cataloged in detail in his 1899 publication.[69] Charles Ramsdell spoke in 1901 on the same topic:

> *If one cannot afford to buy the more expensive nursery stock, there are the native plants of the woods to fall back upon. The utility of collected natives in landscape work is little appreciated. Many shrubs are classed as brush by the average person, and accordingly grubbed out as weeds. But, if notice were taken of them at various*

seasons and their peculiarities studied, there would be very few but what would be desirable, if used rightly.[70]

Manning's philosophy of utilizing native plants within the landscape was again emphasized by Ramsdell:

> *[T]he vegetation growing on [the home site] should be noted and left untouched for a time. After careful observation, the undesirable ones can be taken out and others added. Many beautiful trees and shrubs are removed by the grader in obtaining a level surface. I heard of a case once, where the owner "brushed," as he called it, a beautiful little valley full of native plants, then called in a landscape gardener for advice to improve it, and was much surprised to find that he advised the use of the very same kinds that the owner had so industriously grubbed out.*[71]

✦ WILLIAM TOOLE ✦

William Toole was an active member of the Wisconsin State Horticultural Society from 1880 until his death in 1926, and a contributor at every meeting during this period. He served on the WSHS executive board for twenty-six years, holding the office of president on two occasions.[1] At his nursery in Baraboo, Garry-nee-Dule—Gaelic for gardens of the O'Tooles—he developed and grew more than eighty varieties of pansies for commercial florists. But his real love was for the wild flowers of the Wisconsin prairie. As a member of the Chicago-based organization Friends of Our Native Landscape, he interacted with proponents of the emerging Prairie style of landscape design, including Jens Jensen, O. C. Simonds, and Wilhelm Miller. Toole was an advocate of the use of native plants in the home landscape long before their use became fashionable: he not only grew and sold varieties that he had propagated from the wild but also frequently promoted their advantages in WSHS articles and lectures throughout the state.[2] In 1922 five of his papers on this topic were published as *Native Plants of Wisconsin Suitable for Cultivation*.

NOTES

1. "William Toole, 1841–1926" *Wisconsin Horticulture* 16, no. 9 (May 1926), 126.

2. Huron H. Smith, "Wisconsin's Burbank," *Wisconsin Horticulture* 13, no. 2 (October 1922), 22.

Baraboo horticulturist and pansy grower William Toole was another WSHS member who promoted the use of native plants. His membership in the Chicago-based organization Friends of Our Native Landscape gave him the opportunity to transmit and disperse information and suggestions from that organization to WSHS members.[72] His suggested native shrubs for Wisconsin gardens was included for the first time in the WSHS recommended varieties list in 1904.

The influence of Toole, along with the development of what Wilhelm Miller referred to as the "prairie spirit in landscape gardening," may have helped give Wisconsin its reputation as a leader in the native landscape movement. Certainly, the use of native plants was highly encouraged in WSHS publications during the early decades of the twentieth century.

Reading the often fervent words of these Wisconsin gardeners in WSHS publications, it's easy to imagine their concerns and dreams as they settled in their new communities and tried to create their "ideal" homes and gardens. Certainly, nostalgia must have played a part, as they optimistically struggled to create order within a strange and somewhat unfriendly landscape. Their reliance on nationally published literature is obvious, but it is interesting to follow the presentations and articles of the emerging leaders of this group—both men and women—as they gradually developed their own voices to translate national trends into more regionally appropriate suggestions for Wisconsin garden composition, including layout, boundaries, and placement of vegetation. The next step was to build on this framework with recommendations of the most suitable types of plants that would not only survive the harshness of Wisconsin's climate and its varied terrain but also reflect the artistic abilities of their owners.

Graceful Vines and Sweet Wild Roses: Recommended Plants

*When the door yard of every farm house is neatly fenced in, the fence whitewashed,
and covered with vines; beds of flowers, and stands and rustic vases blooming with
beauty; every old tree trunk covered with mosses and vines, hiding its unseemingly
proportions; then shall we find neatness and order assuming its place in the interior
of the house; the tired mother will find rest in the brightness around her;
the young people will have something to interest them at home, and even the wee
little ones in their play gardens can enjoy "loving flowers."*

MRS. D. C. AYERS, 1879[1]

Clearing the land and building a home was just the first step in creating
"home grounds." In the opinion of the Wisconsin State Horticultural Society,
the homeowner then needed to carefully consider the form and placement
of boundaries, trees, and lawns so as to create a canvas on which to paint the landscape
elements considered necessary for a contented and successful existence. This idealistic
goal was the base of the WSHS philosophy, although both the canvas and the picture it
contained underwent several changes between 1869 and 1930.

Painting the canvas meant planting trees, shrubs, flowers, and vines. WSHS
speakers enthusiastically addressed this topic during this sixty-year period, with
approximately one hundred and fifty presentations on "what to plant" appearing in

WSHS publications. As a result of this interest, beginning in 1886, annual recommended varieties lists for trees, shrubs, and flowers were added to the already extensive fruit tree lists that appeared in each issue of the *Transactions of the Wisconsin State Horticultural Society* and the society's published annual reports. The lists are simply recommendations and as such cannot be used to document what was actually planted in individual gardens. However, they are a very useful supplementary research tool because their content mirrors the changing ideals for the Wisconsin garden and the availability and subsequent popularity of specific plants. Annual flowers and vegetables generally were not included as part of the lists, although in 1917 the WSHS published a separate pamphlet on recommended vegetables for war gardens.

By 1870 Wisconsin gardeners could purchase a wide variety of seeds and plants from itinerant peddlers, local nurseries, mail-order catalogs, or the general store. Garden historian Sharon D. Crawford traced the history of the developing market for regional suppliers of seeds and plants during the early and mid-nineteenth century and found that by 1850 approximately fifty nurseries were already established in Wisconsin.[2] Of these, about thirty were still in existence in the late 1860s and most were located in the southern third of the state. By 1920 approximately fifty nurseries were advertising in the monthly issues of *Wisconsin Horticulture*, offering specialized varieties of numerous plants, shrubs, and trees. Advertisements for landscape needs began to appear in the journal after the turn of the twentieth century.

The national interest in gardening had created a strong market for garden equipment, with lawn mowers, watering systems, and an increasing array of chemicals easing everyday maintenance. Horticultural societies, garden clubs, and civic improvement projects had helped to turn gardening into a fashionable social activity. In Wisconsin, WSHS membership peaked at three thousand in 1930, with twenty-four active garden clubs reporting to *Wisconsin Horticulture*.

These colorful nasturtiums grace the cover of the John A. Salzer Seed Company's 1919 catalog. The La Crosse nursery operation was founded in 1868 and by 1892 had $1 million in annual sales.

WHI IMAGE ID 68361

The Coe, Converse & Edwards Co. nursery was one of the first to include landscape design in its advertisements.

WISCONSIN HORTICULTURE, DECEMBER 1915

One of the many homes our Landscape Department has helped to make attractive.

We are now ready to help you make your place a Beauty Spot.

A booklet showing places we have planned and planted is free.

You want the best varieties when planting your Orchard, Home Grounds or Fruit Garden. Our catalogue tells you about them.

The Coe, Converse & Edwards Co., Nurserymen, Fort Atkinson, Wis.

As would be expected based on the population distribution of Wisconsin residents, the primary emphasis in the early recommended varieties lists was on utility trees and shrubs that would serve as windbreaks, boundary elements, animal barriers, and timber for the farmstead. Ornamental plants were originally limited to a few suggested shrubs and roses, but the evolution of their importance in the home landscape can be traced in the lists as they received increasing amounts of space. There is a strong correlation between plants on the lists and those recommended by speakers at preceding annual meetings, raising the likelihood that member input influenced the contents. The WSHS also reported on ornamental plants grown on its test site at the College of Agriculture grounds at the University of Wisconsin.

The lists were published annually from 1886 to 1928. Updates and revisions were made every few years to include new categories of plants that had been judged suitable for Wisconsin home grounds.[3] By 1928 the original one-page list was a cumbersome ten-page pamphlet with numerous categories that, according to its editors, needed extensive revision.[4] In April 1930 a rather different list appeared in *Wisconsin Horticulture,* under the title "Planning the Flower Garden: Varieties Recommended for Wisconsin by Special Committee."[5] Interestingly, this list is composed entirely of perennial flowers, categorized by size, color, time of bloom, and sun/shade requirements, with the stated goal of providing as long a season of color as possible. This new emphasis suggests that the journal's readership now had the leisure time for serious ornamental gardening for pleasure rather than necessity.

The reasoning behind the publication of the recommended varieties lists (see appendix) was explained, either indirectly or directly, by speakers at annual meetings or in WSHS publications. The original articles make fascinating reading, mostly because of the detailed descriptions in which authors freely revealed their personal successes and failures in their gardens. They praised or condemned particular trees, shrubs, or flower varieties, advised on planting and maintenance techniques, and relayed national landscaping ideals to their audience. From a historical perspective, these writings are invaluable: Taken as a whole, their content traces the changing styles of the Wisconsin home landscape, thus providing the modern gardener with the context and tools to re-create or restore an accurate vintage garden. Individually, they reveal the everyday joys and frustrations of Wisconsin gardeners, both amateur and professional, as they endeavored to improve and beautify their home grounds, school yards, or city streets. The background for the recommended lists is described in the following sections.

Evergreen Trees

Thirteen varieties of evergreens, including pine and spruce, were recommended for "general" or "ornamental" planting in 1886, and several varieties of low-growing juniper were added to the list in 1893. In 1894 the evergreen list was subdivided into four groups, based on suitability for each use: windbreaks, hedges and screens, lawns and cemeteries, and small lawns.

Windbreaks and hedges provided shelter, protection, and privacy on the rural farmstead. As early as 1872, George J. Kellogg of Janesville argued that the cost of planting one thousand Norway spruce to form a windbreak around a homestead was well worth the cost of a colt (which he priced at ninety-five dollars). "Just stop and think how the wind feels [through] your fluttering garments when there are no evergreens on these broad prairies of the west. . . . It needs no better argument than this to prove their 'beauty and utility.'"[6] And in 1878 the honorable A. A. Arnold criticized the comments made by farmers that evergreens were too expensive, too time-consuming, or too difficult to grow, stating that he had no patience with such excuses. "For me," he noted, "I would have, if I could, a forest of them. . . . In a forest of evergreens, the cold winds could not penetrate, nor the hot sun invade."[7] Arnold recommended buying nursery trees rather than replanting forest ones, which he thought had a poor chance of survival out of their natural habitat. Like many other speakers, he recommended Norway, balsam, or black spruce for windbreaks, interspersed with juniper, cedar, and pine. White cedar (American arborvitae) was preferable for hedges but should be trimmed and sheared. (See page 55 for a view of windbreak rows of evergreens enclosing an entire farmstead.)

By 1898 the "stiff, regular rows" of a windbreak were considered "awkward and angular" by horticulturist W. D. Boynton of Shiocton. He suggested that a softer, more graceful appearance formed by grouping mixed evergreens in a "sort of oblong, half circle" would be more appealing.[8]

The 1894 addition of the "small lawn" category of evergreens to the recommended list correlates with the increased attention to the urban and suburban garden. Large evergreens on city lawns were discouraged because they hid the house from the street and became ungainly and difficult to prune. In 1898 W. D. Boynton suggested that an arborvitae hedge would make a suitable background for an urban lawn when comprised of "single specimens . . . selected from varieties that have a compact and symmetrical habit of growth, such as the Blue Spruce . . . the Red Cedar and other members of the Juniper family."[9] In 1920 several new varieties of small evergreens were added to the list, and categorization reverted to size rather than application in the landscape. The additional varieties of ornamental evergreens included dwarf juniper, globe arborvitae, and Hovey's golden arborvitae—all popular additions to foundation plantings.

Throughout the time period, pine, spruce, and arborvitae continued to be favorite choices, probably because of their known reliability in the climate and soils of Wisconsin.

Deciduous Trees

In 1886 the recommended list included a wide variety of deciduous trees. Weeping varieties of birch and willow, as well as ash and poplar trees, were strongly favored for lawn planting, while larger trees such as elm, maple, basswood, and linden were preferred for street shade. During the first few years the recommendations were published, deciduous trees suitable for timber were listed, but in 1894 this category was removed, leaving two groups of deciduous trees, classified as suitable for either cemeteries or lawns. Lawn plantings by this time included most trees previously suggested for timber, such as maple and oak, and newly listed varieties like the Kentucky coffee tree and *Catalpa spicrosa*.

In 1904 the most desirable large deciduous trees were designated with double stars; American elm, green ash, linden, and some maples were the most highly recommended, though their specific use was not mentioned. Box elder was listed as a desirable deciduous lawn tree rather than as a timber tree for the first time. A new category of "deciduous Ornamental trees" still included most of the previously listed weeping varieties, with the addition of Russian mulberry. Six years later two varieties of crab apples were added, but, apart from this, the list remained the same until 1920, when it was revised and reordered into three categories: "Large Deciduous Trees," "For Streets and Highways," and "Small Deciduous Trees." The last group was considered ornamental rather than useful either for "shade or defense."

The size of a mature Norway maple made it a popular choice for a street tree.

WISCONSIN HORTICULTURE,
APRIL 1917

At that time, twenty-four deciduous trees were listed in the first category, and four of these—American elm, Norway maple, linden, and pin oak—were recommended for street and highway planting. The area between the sidewalk and the road, sometimes known as the terrace or parkway, was a popular location for these favorites because of their ease of maintenance, quality of shade, and beauty at maturity. Municipalities eventually took over street tree planning and planting, but the variety and placement of trees in street scenes from the late 1800s indicate that individual homeowners had free rein over the variety and number of trees planted in this area.[10]

By 1920 the "Small Deciduous Trees" list no longer included weeping varieties of willow and birch, which had been popular in the late 1800s; additions included native plants such as juneberry, hawthorn, and buckeye. This correlates with the declining interest in formal geometric layouts, which in the Victorian era had included specimen trees in the lawn, and the increasing use of native species.

Latin terminology was added in 1920, probably to match the style used in national publications and to reinforce the focus on professionalism in WSHS. The deciduous tree list remained unchanged between 1920 and 1930.

This circa 1890 photograph illustrates street planting along a very wide terrace or parkway in Madison. Notice the double row of trees—probably American elm—on the terrace. Homes are built close to the street, with boardwalks leading to the front door. Most of the small lawns are unfenced with an occasional shrub or small tree in the yard. Most city streets lost their wide terraces and large shade trees to road-widening projects and Dutch elm disease that transformed the residential landscape during the mid-twentieth century.

WHI IMAGE ID 67918

Shrubs

Between 1886 and 1925 the shrub category showed the largest increase in size. In 1886 the hardy shrub list included lilac (*Syringa*), upright strawberry tree (*Euonymus*), smoke tree, and a few others. Half-hardy shrubs suitable for home planting included weigela and hydrangea. By 1894 shrubs were specifically designated for cemetery planting as well, and further subdivided into those suitable for lawns, screens, or hedges. Varieties of barberry were added in 1886, but the overall number of shrubs in the category was still quite small.

In 1893 Milwaukee nurseryman James Currie presented an enthusiastic report on varieties of hardy shrubs for the Wisconsin garden, including old favorites and new additions.[11] He encouraged grouping mixed varieties of shrubs under trees, as hedges, and to divide various parts of the garden, but he strongly advised against indiscriminate pruning into balls or cones. "When pruning is done," he noted, "see that the shrub still preserves its . . . looseness and grace of form, which with care and judgment may easily be done."[12]

In 1904 the list was revised to include new varieties of dogwood, hydrangea, weigela, and honeysuckle, bringing the total number of recommended shrubs to thirty. Latin nomenclature was added at this time and a new category—shrub height—was

Like many garden writers of the early twentieth century, Eben Rexford recommended *Spiraea x vanhouttei* for its graceful shape.

THE MAKING OF A HOME, 1916

Spireas of all varieties have retained their appeal to this day. Here, *Spiraea x vanhouttei* is in bloom in Door County.

LEE SOMERVILLE

incorporated. It is likely that this sudden increased focus was a result of the growing national interest in shrubs as part of small garden design, the use of shrubs for foundation plantings, and a corresponding increase in availability from local and regional nurseries. The appointment of Frederic Cranefield as executive secretary of the WSHS in 1904 initiated a greater emphasis on ornamental planting in the home grounds and likely also played a role in the increased popularity of shrubs.

Beginning in 1906, the WSHS published a "Black List" that contained shrubs thought to be unsuitable for the Wisconsin climate. According to the accompanying explanation, these shrubs had been "tested on the grounds of the Experiment Station at Madison and found unsatisfactory."[13] An additional note stated that although some grew well, they would not blossom without winter protection.[14] In 1920 the list was amended to read "Shrubs needing winter protection." The list included azaleas, privet, daphne, and some flowering fruit shrubs. That such a list was kept shows that the WSHS was actively trying to grow and maintain ornamental shrubs as well as fruit trees at its test site. It also underlines the growing interest in small ornamental shrubs at the beginning of the twentieth century.

In 1915 a separate "List of Native Shrubs Desirable for Planting on the Home Grounds" was included in the section. This is a notable addition because it documents the rising interest in native species in early-twentieth-century Wisconsin. The thirty-five varieties were apparently chosen for their ease of transplanting and maintenance. A much larger list is given in Warren H. Manning's 1899 *A Handbook for Planning and Planting Small Home Grounds* and in William Toole's *Native Plants of Wisconsin Suitable for Cultivation*, a collection of articles published by the WSHS in 1922.[15] Varieties included sumac, wild roses, dogwood, and other species.

Annual and Perennial Flowers

Flowers, both annual and perennial, were a popular topic at WSHS meetings; with the exception of the rose, however, this interest was not translated into inclusion on the recommended lists until 1915, when two new categories of plants were added. "Six Hardy Herbaceous Perennials" recommended phlox, peony, larkspur, bleeding heart, lily of the valley, and daylily, with iris and poppy added the following year; "Spring Flowering Bulbs" included varieties of tulips, narcissus, and crocus. From this date onward, varieties of perennials and bulbs were listed; recommended native perennials were included beginning in 1915.

No official recommended lists were ever produced for annual flowers, although their use in the home landscape was often discussed at meetings between 1870 and

This circa 1910 image shows the home and garden of Martin M. Secor, mayor of Racine between 1884 and 1888, and founder of the Northwestern Trunk and Traveling Bag Manufactory. The neat edging, wide pathways, and geometrically shaped beds contain a mass of well-maintained rose bushes and other flowers that contrast with the softer foundation plantings and porch vines framing the large Italianate home.

WHI IMAGE ID 40002

1890. Favorite varieties included pansies, verbenas, nasturtiums, annual phlox, coleus, sweet peas, stocks, and balsam. Tall exotics such as amaranth, ricinus, caladiums, and geraniums were popularly used in tropical beds cut into the lawn. (See illustration on page 6.) Typically, speakers would list their favorite annuals along with the reasons why they planted them in their gardens, as in this example from 1875:

> *Of course we will have our Annuals, Sweet Alyssum, Candy-Tuft, Phlox, Mignonette, the modest Browallia, and Nemophilia.*[16] *. . . The new varieties of Tropaeolums [nasturtium] are showy and handsome. . . . The new Double-Balsams are perfect, and the white, almost as beautiful as a Rose. The Convolvulus Minor must not be neglected on account of its old-fashioned relative, the Morning-Glory, which a place should be provided for, if only to please the children. . . . [And] do not forget the Sweet Pea.*
>
> *If one has a large lawn, a few beds cut in it can be made very effective . . . Caladium Esculentum is a good plant for such purposes. . . . One bed filled with*

The peony has stood the test of time in Wisconsin gardens. Even though they were considered old-fashioned in 1911, peonies were still recommended as something that "ought to be in every Garden."

WISCONSIN HORTICULTURE,
MAY 1911

Sisson's Peony Gardens was the highlight of the tiny village of Rosendale from 1929 until the 1980s. The garden, originally part of a nursery operation, has recently been restored. Although it is no longer a nursery, old varieties of peonies are still available to view.

EMAJEAN WESTPHAL

Large annuals such as the castor bean plant were a Victorian favorite because of their quick growth and dramatic leaves. During the late 1800s they were often used in tropical beds, or, as in this example, trained over supports to create a shady bower.
HOME FLORICULTURE, 1903

This color illustration of bedding plants included coleus and *Pyrethrum aurea*.
VICK'S MONTHLY MAGAZINE, NOVEMBER 1881

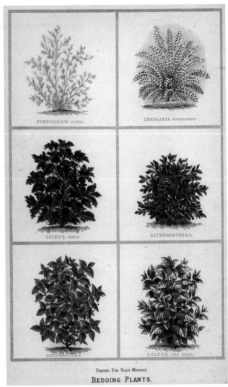

Coleus Verschaffeltii *or* Achyranthus, *and another with any of the varieties of white-leaf plants, will be quite attractive.*[17]

Mrs. D. C. Ayers suggested the following annuals for a beginner's garden in 1877:

If four friends purchase together, twenty kinds of seeds can be procured for one dollar and divided, giving a large supply to each one. We would recommend to beginners to select Candytuft, Petunia, Phlox-Drummondi, Mignonette, Pinks, Pansies and Asters. . . . If you have old kegs, pails and pans, set them around the ground in the front of the house, cover them with bark from the wood pile, old grape vines and moss, fill them with earth. . . . [In the woods] you may find vines; bitter sweet, woodbines, perennial peas, and many a one unnamed save in Indian lore. Gather them in with ferns and grasses, and you will have what many in the cities pay large prices for.[18]

Dr. H. Allen, whose ornate design for a flower garden was discussed in the preceding chapter, suggested filling the beds with a wide variety of annuals:

The centre bed we will fill entirely with verbenas, or if you choose a variegated canna may be put in the centre, and around this a circle of dark colored verbenas; next a circle of pure white, alternated with pink. The outer circle will be composed of a tastefully arranged variety of colors, all comprising from 20 to 24 plants. . . . You will next have a bed of Geraniums and Lantanas with a double white Fever few in the centre. A bed of Pelargoniums, silver-leaved and "horse shoe," with double scarlet and pink and a Lady Washington. The first bed you will have supplied from the green-house each spring, or from the conservatory, or plant window of your own dwelling. . . . You want an entire bed of Double Portulaca. This is best grown in a mass; another of Phlox Drummondi; a third of petunias, dark shades, a fourth of Mirabilis (or 4 o'clock). . . . Sweet Peas and Zinnias and Euphorbia and Datura, you will plant in the border. . . . You will, of course, have a place for the Pansies, those intelligent, half-speaking faces, which always look at you so wishfully. Everybody also has Asters and Balsams, and Dahlias and Tulips; but the Gladiolus and Tuberose are not so common, yet are easily raised, and a bed of them will please you well.[19]

This amount of detail and order was not typical of speakers' recommendations.

Rexford encouraged readers to plant whatever was left over in a special bed—the "odds and ends corner."
AMATEUR GARDENCRAFT, 1912

The 'Wisconsin Red' dahlia, formerly known as 'Catherine Becker'. The origin of this vintage dahlia was researched by Victoria Dirst and the growers at Old House Gardens in Ann Arbor, Michigan, who identified it as one that had been grown in the Wausaukee and Marinette areas since the 1940s. VICTORIA DIRST

Annuals were often used in various types of containers, such as garden vases, baskets, window boxes, and old tree stumps. Suitable plants depended on the location of the container, as noted in this excerpt from an 1877 presentation:

> *For the shady spots there are so many beautiful things that come within the reach of all—Ferns, Ivys, Lobelia, Maurandya, Smilax, Fuchsia, Vinca, Begonia, Cocolobia, Artillery Plant, and Coleus,—it is really hard to know where to stop. It is much more difficult to find plants to do well fully exposed to the sun. Brasella Rubra, or variegated Madeira vine (this is of shrubby nature), stands the heat admirably, growing handsomer as the heat increases; also any of the Centaurea, Artemesia, Gnaphalium, Geranium, Alternanthera, and Tritoma. For a trailing plant, the old Moneywort must not be overlooked. . . . Kenilworth Ivy also fills a basket well. It is light and graceful. Those who are so fortunate as to live in easy access to the woods can or should have no excuse for not beautifying their grounds, for certainly nature has filled Wisconsin's woods with living wealth of loveliness in vines, flowers and ferns.*[20]

At the annual state fairs, premiums were awarded to nonprofessional growers of varieties such as verbena, annual phlox, petunia, and pansies, as well as dahlias and gladioli. As the fashion for massed annual bedding declined, there appears to have been a corresponding increase in the use of perennials, especially in borders around the front lawn or interspersed with shrubs. Several speakers suggested that annuals could be intermixed with vegetables if no other planting space was available or placed in cutting beds behind the house.[21]

Annuals and perennials were usually discussed in talks with titles such as "What Flowers to Plant"—a popular topic between 1869 and 1930. In 1915 two groups of perennials were listed separately, the first being a general list and the second devoted to native perennials suitable for home planting. Most of the plants on the first list had been discussed or recommended to members in previous talks or articles. New varieties were added at times, but the list remained essentially unchanged throughout the decade. The herbaceous border, consisting entirely of perennials, continued to be a popular landscape choice between 1900 and 1930.

Speakers weren't the only ones to put forth their opinions on what to plant. The informal character of *Wisconsin Horticulture* encouraged reader interaction, as illustrated by the following 1914 response to a Milwaukee reader's request for a border planting that would furnish constant color:

Above left: An attractive perennial border. The caption that originally accompanied this image noted that "both perennials and biennials help make possible this attractive feature of the home."
WISCONSIN HORTICULTURE, FEBRUARY 1928

Above right: A modern example of a prairie garden with native Wisconsin plants at Heritage Flower Farm in Mukwonago
BETTY ADELEMAN

If this was my border, here is what I would set:

10 Delphinium Formosum Hybridum	*5 Tiger Lilies*
20 Hardy Phlox assorted colors	*5 Shasta Daisies*
20 Pyrethrum Roseum assorted colors	*5 Dicentra Spectabilis*
5 Single Hollyhocks assorted colors	*10 Aquilegia assorted colors*
5 Aster, Nova anglea	*10 Double Russian Violets*
5 Oriental Poppies	*10 Platycodon blue and white*
5 Boltonia Latisquama	*5 Ranunculus, Acris, Fl. Pl.*
5 Lemon Lilies	*5 Primula Officinalis*
5 German Iris assorted colors	*5 Dianthus Plumaris, Fl. Pl.*
5 Achillea the Pearl	*5 Iris Nudicale*

Set the Delphinium, Hollyhocks, Boltonia, Oriental Poppies, Tiger Lillies and New England Asters in the center of the border and around the edge of the border plant the Violets, Pyrtheum, Platycodon, Dwarf Iris, Shasta Daisies, Pinks and Primroses running the Phlox, German Iris, Lemon Lilies, Bleeding Heart, Bachelor Buttons, Columbine and Achille just back of the border row.

The Mendota Beach bulb garden of Mr. and Mrs. E. L. Roloff in Madison
WISCONSIN HORTICULTURE, MAY 1930

Below: This curved border of "old breeder" tulips, including 'Cri de Coeur,' graces the side garden of the Yawkey House Museum in Wausau.
LYNN BUHMANN

A lovely herbaceous border with lupines in the foreground surrounds a neatly manicured lawn. Note the rustic trellises.
WISCONSIN HORTICULTURE, MARCH 1919

A field of lupines in an abandoned Door County meadow
LEE SOMERVILLE

> *The one hundred and fifty plants properly grown in a forty foot border will give the owner the greatest of pleasure as no matter what time he may look upon it he will find some flower in bloom that will interest him from the earliest days in spring until late in the fall.*[22]

Very little information is given on varieties of bulbs or tuberous plants, although talks on their growth habits and beauty were occasional topics. For choices on suitable varieties for the heirloom garden, we must go to period bulb catalogs or texts such as Denise Wiles Adams's *Restoring American Gardens: An Encyclopedia of Heirloom Ornamental Plants, 1640–1940*.[23]

Roses

Roses were popular ornamentals for American gardens from earliest settlement days. Wisconsin gardeners were no less enthusiastic according to WSHS records. Numerous talks extolled the beauty of this "exquisite combination of perfume, form and color."[24] The 1886 list included a category for roses; this list continued in expanded form until 1925. Despite the national interest in introducing new varieties to the American public, early WSHS favorites persisted. The 1886 recommended list consisted of climbers, moss roses, and hybrid perpetuals. Briar roses and hardy garden roses were added as separate categories in 1894 and 1915, respectively.

The tremendous national interest in roses led to the formation of the American Rose Society in 1892. Thanks to the growth and development of the rose industry in the United States and Europe, members of the WSHS had plenty of options among the roses recommended by the organization's horticulturists. The total number of recommended roses during the six decades covered in this book is forty-five; however, not all of these remained on the lists for the entire period. Persistent varieties in the climber category were 'Gem of the Prairies', 'Prairie Queen', 'Seven Sisters', and 'Russell's Cottage'. The enduring moss rose variety favorites were 'Salet', 'Perpetual White Moss', 'Deuil de Paul Fontaine', and 'Henri Martin'. Hybrid perpetuals formed the largest group of recommended varieties, in spite of their need for winter protection. Some of the long-standing fragrant roses in this group include the delicate pink 'Mrs. John Laing', the crimson 'American Beauty', the deep pink 'Magna Charta', and 'Vick's Caprice', a pink-and-white-striped sport (a genetic mutation) discovered by the James Vick Seed Company in 1881. Modern gardeners can still find most of these old roses at specialty nurseries.[25]

Left: These hardy rambler roses were offered for sale in 1919 by the John A. Salzer Seed Company, which claimed that these three varieties—'Dorothy Perkins', 'Crimson Rambler', and 'Yellow Rambler'—would grow up to fifteen feet in a year and be unsurpassed for brilliance of color and amount of blooms.
WHI IMAGE ID 79903

Right: The 'Apothecary Rose' (*Rosa gallica officinalis*) next to the Victorian bandstand at Heritage Hill State Historical Park in Green Bay.
JIM DOCKENDORFF

Vines

Climbing vines were a ubiquitous decorative element in the Wisconsin vernacular garden throughout the late nineteenth and early twentieth centuries. They provided needed shade for porches and verandas but were also considered to be highly attractive and ornamental. Numerous presentations praised their use, and archival photographs illustrate their popularity.

The WSHS annual lists of recommended trees and shrubs included vines from the start. For the first few years they were listed as "climbers" under the shrub list, but they were later listed separately. The most popular hardy vines were two varieties of the fast-growing *Parthenocissus*, known as *Ampelopsis* to early horticulturists: American ivy (*Parthenocissus quinquefolia* or *Ampelopsis quinquefolia*) is a native vine, also known as Virginia creeper or Engelmann ivy; Boston ivy (*Parthenocissus tricuspidata* or *Ampelopsis tricuspidata*) was introduced into America from Japan in the 1860s and quickly became a favorite. Early speakers did not always differentiate between the two ivy varieties, as they showed similar growth habits, hardiness, and vibrant fall color.

Other popular recommendations were various forms of clematis, grape ivy, and honeysuckle. Annual vines mentioned by speakers included nasturtiums and morning glories.

Eben Rexford loved all kinds of vines including some, such as kudzu, that are now known to be highly invasive. In his books are numerous photographs and sketches of vines climbing exuberantly along fences, up porch supports and roofs, or on trellises. He recommended several varieties of clematis, honeysuckle, and *Ampelopsis* for perennial vines, and, for fillers, annuals such as sweet peas, nasturtiums, and morning glories.
AMATEUR GARDENCRAFT, 1912

Honeysuckle and nasturtiums abound, offering shade, color, and beauty on this wide front porch.
AMATEUR GARDENCRAFT, 1912

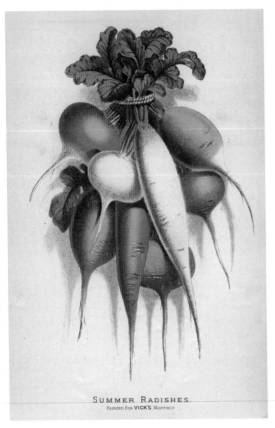

SUMMER RADISHES.
PAINTED FOR VICK'S MONTHLY

This bouquet of summer radishes that graced the March 1881 frontispiece of *Vick's Monthly Magazine* differs from the periodical's usual cover art of colorful flower arrangements—perhaps hinting that vegetables had then become an accepted addition to the home garden.

Vegetables

Although the topic of vegetable varieties, especially those grown for home use, was much less popular than that of ornamental plants, speakers occasionally reported on the best varieties to be grown at home. In 1892 Mrs. J. Montgomery Smith of Mineral Point spoke about growing lettuce, peas, beans, and corn in her garden, and the use of a hotbed to start warm-weather plants such as tomatoes, eggplant, cauliflower, broccoli, celery, and okra.[26] Her paper gave rise to an observation, by a J. S. Harris, that he had traveled "around a good deal, and the only fruit [he had] found on the table among farmers was cabbage and all the fruit many of them grew was cabbage and pumpkins."[27]

Occasional letters and articles in *The Wisconsin Horticulturist* and *Wisconsin Horticulture* suggested favorite varieties of vegetables and fruits, but it was not until the threat of war and a perceived food shortage that the WSHS seriously began to encourage home vegetable gardens, known as war gardens and, later, victory gardens. In 1919 several "War Garden Circulars" issued jointly by the WSHS and the Extension Office of the University of Wisconsin College of Agriculture and aimed at the beginning gardener, covered such topics as "Getting Ready for the Garden," "Garden Soils and Garden Making," and "Protect Your Garden."[28] A list of recommended varieties of beans, beets, cabbage, carrots, lettuce, onions, parsnip, peas, radishes, rutabaga, spinach, tomatoes, and turnips for the home garden appeared in the February 1919 edition of *Wisconsin Horticulture*. Among the "best" were Crosby's Egyptian beet, the Chantenay carrot, and Bloomsdale Savoy spinach.

Evergreen and deciduous trees had the most longevity on the recommended lists. There was little change in suggested varieties, although their location on the home lot underwent modification, possibly as a result of their unexpected size at maturity.

The varieties of shrubs increased dramatically after the turn of the century, as their use was recommended for foundation planting in front of the house and in lieu of

Striking companions at Heritage Flower Farm include 'Autumn Joy' sedum, which was introduced to American gardeners prior to the 1920s by Germany's George Arends Nursery, and blue mistflower.

BETTY ADELMAN

fencing along the sides of the lot. In 1870 shrubs were primarily recommended only for cemetery planting, but photographs from WSHS publications, especially *Wisconsin Horticulture*, and the Eben Rexford books indicate that old favorites like the spireas and lilacs retained their popularity well into the twentieth century.

The varieties of perennial flowers, vines, and roses did not change much between 1869 and 1930. Perennial plants were massed in borders along walks and driveways to create season-long color and texture. As the fashion for carpet bedding waned, WSHS members usually recommended annuals be placed in separate cutting beds behind the house or in containers and window boxes rather than in ornamental beds.

In general, however, the varieties of plants in the Wisconsin vernacular garden changed less than did the patterns in which they were planted. The exception is in the marked increase of native shrubs and plants after 1900, the advantages of which were widely touted by such proponents as Warren H. Manning, WSHS executive board members Frederic Cranefield and William Toole, and other regional landscape architects, environmentalists, and ecologists from the academic community.

While reading the literature of the period it's easy to sense the excitement of these amateur and professional gardeners and horticulturists as they explored the possibilities of gardening—in new surroundings or on familiar ground—shared their experiences, and traded their knowledge. As they planted trees, shrubs, flowers, and vines around their homes they were also putting down roots in their communities. Like today, their membership in state, regional, or local horticultural societies no doubt fueled their interest and increased their desire to create more beautiful surroundings. Many of the plants they grew are available today, providing the historical gardener with a vast array of wonderful choices.

In the Wisconsin Garden—
Yesterday and Today

"In the garden!" What picture does this phrase bring to your mind? . . .
Do you think only a few straggling flowers, a few sickly vegetables, untidy walks and
ill-kept beds? No. Is it not true that the phrase brings to mind a garden in its
perfection, without thought of the labor and care necessary thereto? Thereby proving
that in this direction the result so far exceeds the labor put forth, that in the glory
of the achievement all thought of the effort is lost.

MRS. HELEN H. CHARLTON, 1892[1]

Like other speakers of the era, Brodhead gardener Helen H. Charlton envisioned the garden as a symbol for life, suggesting that hard work leads to mental and spiritual perfection, which she saw expressed as beauty and order in the landscape. While today's gardeners may not delve as deeply into these philosophical ideals, they still find satisfaction, happiness, and sometimes peace while digging, pruning, and weeding "in the garden."

If you are interested in creating or maintaining a vintage garden, it's not just about physical labor. Unearthing the history of your own garden or the ones in your community is an intriguing project—one that can serendipitously reveal previously unknown facts about earlier inhabitants and their lifestyles. Photographs, letters, journals, maps, and publications usually available at local or regional libraries and historical societies

Opposite page, clockwise from top left: This is the type of rural garden that Helen H. Charlton might have been imagining. The original caption accompanying this image of the Wauwatosa home of E. E. Haasch read: "From a sodless hill to this in 3 years."
WISCONSIN HORTICULTURE, MAY 1928

William Toole referenced this photograph to illustrate the use of small native shrubs such as viburnum close to a house if it "stands high."
WISCONSIN HORTICULTURE, SEPTEMBER 1914

This deep herbaceous border with the neat lawn framing it is much more typical of the type of home landscape recommended for "farm or city" gardens.
WISCONSIN HORTICULTURE, MAY 1916

can be a starting point for researching a particular garden. The Wisconsin State Horticultural Society publications are available in the University of Wisconsin–Madison libraries and also online. They are intriguing documents that capture the voices of Wisconsin residents from all parts of the state, spanning several decades. The Wisconsin Historical Society has a vast array of photographs, many of which are also available for online viewing.[2]

As I researched this book, it became obvious that there was no such thing as a "typical" Wisconsin garden during the late nineteenth and early twentieth centuries. A vernacular garden, by definition, is unique. It adapts and changes as a result of a combination of factors such as family and community traditions, neighborhood expectations, economic feasibility, availability of horticultural literature, or simply personal interests and preferences. It also often contains several layers of ownership and change. But through the publications and photographs available to us, we can at least make an educated guess as to the form and composition of the Wisconsin vintage garden.

The history of an individual house, its occupants, its garden history, and its surroundings should always carry the most weight when designing the form and composition of a vintage garden. Private homeowners have much greater freedom than do historic sites when deciding on layout, plant varieties, and interpretive dates. Many choose to incorporate several layers of style and taste rather than limiting themselves to a precise interpretive date. In *Restoring American Gardens*, Denise Wiles Adams calls this "making-a-new-layer"—one that might retain much of the original layout and vegetation without limiting one's personal vision for the eventual form and function of the garden.[3] Choosing whether to use modern or heirloom varieties of plants and deciding on the layout of the garden and its level of accuracy are purely the homeowner's decisions.

In the case of publicly visited historic gardens, administrators have a responsibility to provide information to the public about the garden, whether or not there are documented interpretive or landscape plans in place. Even if the garden is merely the backdrop to a more fully researched house museum or historic site, it is an integral element of the landscape and therefore in the public eye. Understandably, the garden is sometimes the final and least funded stage of a preservation project, but this is no reason to ignore it when writing the brochures that are handed out to visitors. It is better to simply state that the garden is not yet an accurate representation of the time period, rather than allowing confusion by omission.

For sites with already completed interpretive and landscape plans for their gardens, I recommend making as much information available to visitors as possible, for, based on my experience as a gardener at two historic sites, they are very interested. I've noticed

This plant list provides common names followed by horticultural names for the perennials, current as of June 2008. Annuals, such as marigolds, petunias, cleomes, zinnias, cosmos, coleus, salvia, bachelor buttons, and love lies ableeding, may change from year to year. The map below right identifies each area of the garden by number.

1. SOUTH ENTRANCE
Anthony Waterer Spiraea, *Spiraea x bumalda* 'Anthony Waterer'
Bridal Wreath, *Spiraea x vanhouttei*
Upright Japanese Yew, *Taxus cupidata* 'Capitata'

2. SOUTHWEST CORNER
Daffodils, *Narcissi* 'Red Rascal'
annuals

3. FARWELL FRONT
Bridal Wreath, *Spiraea x vanhouttei*
Lemon Climbing Rose, *Rosa* 'Lemon Meringue'
Shrub Rose, *Rosa* 'J. P. Connel'
Clematis, *Clematis terniflora* 'Sweet Autumn'
Grape Hyacinths/Muscari Mixture:
   M. *armeniacum*, M. *botryoides album*,
   M. *latifolium*, M. *valerie finnis*
Scilla, *S. siberica* 'Spring Beauty'
annuals

4. NORTH SIDE UNDER WINDOWS
Mockorange, *Philadelphus lewisii* 'Blizzard' in memory of Kathy Tank, garden visionary
Hosta, *Hosta*
Ostrich Fern, *Matteuccia pensylvanica*
Common Witchhazel, *Hamelis virginiana*
Dead Nettle, *Lamium maculatum* 'White Nancy' and 'Pewter'
annuals

5. NORTHWEST CORNER
American Basswood, *Tilia americana* 'Redmond'
Dead Nettle, *Lamium maculatum* 'Checkers'
Burning Bush, *Euonymus alata* 'Compacta'
Clematis, *Clematis virginiana*
Daffodils, *Narcissi* 'Ice Follies,' 'King Alfred,' 'Mount Hood,' 'Red Rascal,' 'Salome'
annuals

6. NORTH PARKING LOT EDGE
Shrub Rose, *Rosa rugosa* 'Hansa'
Medora Juniper, *Juniperus scopulorum* 'Medora'
Techny Arborvitae, *Thuja occidentalis* 'Techny'
Hackberry Trees, *Celtis occidentalis*
Butterfly Bush Honeysuckle, *Diervilla sessilifolia* 'Butterfly'
Wild Ginger, *Asarum canadense*
Daffodils, *Narcissi* (See section 5)
Hosta, *Hosta* 'Royal Standard'
Ben Sarek Black Currant, *Ribes* 'Ben Sarek'
annuals

7. NORTHEAST CORNER
Red Lake Currant, *Ribes* 'Red Lake'
Ben Sarek Black Currant, *Ribes* 'Ben Sarek'
Hackberry Tree, *Celtis occidentalis*
Butterfly Bush Honeysuckle, *Diervilla sessilifolia* 'Butterfly'
Purple Lilac, *Syringa vulgaris*
Cream Lilac, *Syringa v.* 'Primrose'
Peony, *Paeonia x lactiflora* 'Festiva Maxima'
Daffodils, *Narcissi* (see section 5)
annuals

8. NORTHEAST ALONG ALLEYWAY
Medora Juniper, *Juniperus scopulorum*, 'Medora'
Red Twig Dogwood, *Cornus sericea*, 'Baileyi'
Gas Plant, *Dictamnus albus*
Allium, A. *azureum*
Peony, *Paeonia* (unknown variety, red)

9. SOUTH ALONG ALLEYWAY
Hackberry Tree, *Celtis occidentalis*
Lily of the Valley, *Convallaria majalis*
Scilla, *S. siberica* 'Spring Beauty'
Grape Hyacinths/Muscari Mixture (see section 3)
Gas Plant, *Dictamnus albus*
Red Twig Dogwood, *Cornus sericea* 'Baileyi'
Snowball Viburnum, *Vibernum opulus* 'Roseum'
Medora Juniper, *Juniperus scopulorum* 'Medora'
Tiger Lily, *Lilium lancifolium*
Daffodils, *Narcissi* (see section 5)
annuals

10. SOUTHEAST CORNER
Clematis, *Clematis virginiana*
John Cabot Climbing Rose, *Rosa* 'John Cabot'
Tall Phlox, *Phlox paniculata* 'David'
Lily, *Lilium asiatic* hybrids by Harold (Hod) Hoepner (unnamed, unknown, and/or unregistered)
Candytuft, *Iberis sempervirens*
Forsythia, *Forsythia x* 'Northern Gold'
Snowdrift Crabapple, *Malus* 'Snowdrift' (in boulevard)

11. SOUTH SIDE ALONG SIDEWALK
Barberry, *Berberis thunbergii* 'Atropurpurea Nana'
White Bleeding Heart, *Dicentra spectabilis* 'Alba'
Daylily, *Hemerocallis lilioasphodelus* 'Iris Perry' and 'Hyperion'
Anthony Waterer Spiraea, *Spiraea x bumalda* 'Anthony Waterer'
Shrub Rose, *Rosa rugosa* 'Blanc Double de Coubert'

12. SOUTH SIDE OF PORCH
Juniper, *Juniperus* (unknown variety)
Anthony Waterer Spiraea, *Spiraea x bumalda* 'Anthony Waterer'
Upright Japanese Yew, *Taxus cupidata* 'Capitata'

Burning Bush

Kim's Knee High

Snowball Viburnum

Dead Nettle

Wild Ginger

Coneflower

Site brochure noting the names and varieties of plants in the Schlegelmilch House garden, owned and operated by the Chippewa Valley Museum, in Eau Claire. Its gardens are representative of the early 1900s. This type of brochure is effective, especially for self-guided tours.
COURTESY OF SCHLEGELMILCH HOUSE

that whenever our group is working, visitors are drawn into the garden with questions about plant varieties and garden layout, or to simply learn about what we are doing. Unfortunately most sites don't have the people power to staff the gardens on a full-time basis and visitors leave without learning as much as they would like. One solution is to make available a comprehensive garden brochure that identifies plant varieties in a useful map.

For those who are in the process of developing a landscape plan for a vintage garden, the following questions help define the scope of the project, whether it will be a professional or in-house project. However, it is important to remember that any historic garden, no matter how accurate, is a representation. It can never be entirely accurate, in part because of the ongoing changes that occur in the ecological and physical environment.

Is there a specific interpretive date for the garden?

Most historic sites or house museums establish an interpretive date or range of dates to highlight the significant events in their history and to attract, engage, and educate the visitor. Typically, the interior furnishings and collections define this time period; ideally, the garden should complement the interpretive date. But the garden is not static: it is a living environment that changes over time. Trees grow, mature, and decline, turning sunny beds shady and vice versa. A shrub that was intended to provide a neat foundation planting can quickly overtake an entire area, while disease and cold winters take their toll on perennial plants and lawns. A garden that was originally intended to have a specific interpretive date can look entirely different twenty years down the road. If possible, establish a range of dates to allow some flexibility in interpretation.

The well-documented elements of the Villa Louis gardens, including various receipts, enable the historic site's staff to portray an accurate example of a high-style, Victorian-era Wisconsin landscape.

WHI IMAGE ID 82655
WHI IMAGE ID 82658

How much archival material is available?

If the garden has been well documented, the research project is much easier. For example, Villa Louis in Prairie du Chien, a Wisconsin Historical Society historic site open to the public, has in its collection an astoundingly detailed record, including receipts, photographs, and maps, of its 1880 landscape plan. Moreover, because this state historic site has retained its integrity, a historic plant inventory identified much of the extant vegetation, including the massive willow trees that grace the grounds.

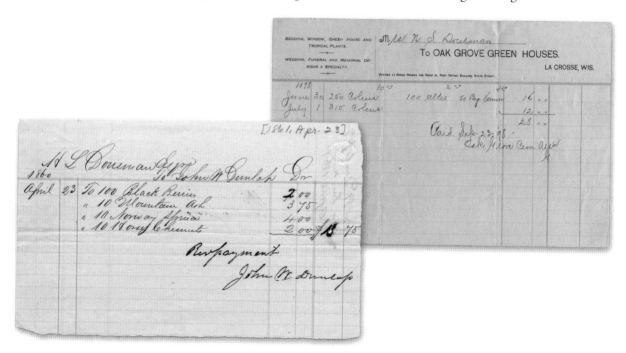

Above left: Dousman family photos in the Wisconsin Historical Society archives offer views of the circa 1898 landscape at Villa Louis, including a tropical bed with canna lilies.
WHI IMAGE ID 81910

Above right: The Yawkey House Museum in Wausau incorporates a formally designed sunken garden and a large decorative pergola.
LYNN BUHMANN

Most sites are not as fortunate. They may have plenty of architectural and family archival material—and even photographs in their collections—but very seldom does that include information on the garden or its contents. Sometimes the historic structure is no longer on its original site and any relationship between the building and its landscape is artificial. Archival sources such as newspapers, local history publications, plat maps, postcards, and bird's-eye-view maps can all help with documentation.

Is there a landscape and/or interpretive plan in place?

The landscape plan will define the form and composition of the garden. It usually documents, in map form, the existing vegetation—varieties of trees, shrubs, and other plants—the hardscaping, and the location of beds. It also defines the short- and long-term plans for the garden, thus clarifying future needs for potential donors.

The interpretive plan determines the narrative of the garden—how it was used and by whom. This is often necessarily an imprecise outline because in many cases there is simply no information about the function of the garden at any particular time. However, even a very nonspecific interpretive plan that incorporates the customs and culture of the region can help provide a focus for the garden and is therefore well worth developing.

Who will determine the methodology and oversee the project?

If your organization has a landscape committee, its members will determine the methodology and oversee the plans for landscape renovations. If your organization does not have a landscape committee, create one so that its members can direct the research and set a timeline for completion.

What are your objectives for the garden?

To determine your ultimate objectives for your vintage garden, you must answer these questions: What is the role of the garden in the context of the site? Is it simply an entryway or will it tell a story? Is it to be a background for outdoor events or a significant interpretive addition in its own right? Let these answers inform all of your other decisions.

How will the research, design blueprint, planting, and ongoing maintenance be funded?

A professional landscape plan for the grounds, drafted by a qualified landscape architect, usually does not include the costs of hardscaping, removal of inappropriate vegetation, the plants and their installation, and, most important, long-term maintenance. All of these must be figured into the final funding requirements.

How much compromise is acceptable?

Developing an accurate vintage garden may require complex, difficult, and unpopular decisions. For example, tree removal may be necessary if a specific interpretive date is planned. Neighbors may object to the appearance of a more accurate but less weed-free and neatly mowed lawn on a residential street. Replacements must be considered for certain varieties of historically recommended trees or plants that are now considered invasive and are either prohibited or not recommended for planting. Furthermore, some historic plants are not easily available, are difficult to grow, or are more expensive than their modern counterparts. It is helpful to identify these potential areas of conflict and compromise in the early stages of the project.

Some compromise is unavoidable and it's important that the visitor be aware of this. For example, the garden of the Kneeland-Walker House in Wauwatosa retains the original outlines of walkways and beds, but modern varieties of plants are used in many cases, with the rationale that this reflects the original owners' intent to showcase new and exciting plants.[4]

Who will look after the garden?

This may be the most important question. A garden committee that commits to the day-to-day maintenance of a historic garden is an invaluable resource. Most of the historic homes and gardens pictured in this chapter have a team of workers—often master gardeners who are knowledgeable, enthusiastic, and generous with their time. Make sure everyone knows exactly what is in the landscape plan and why, and be clear about your expectations.

How will you distribute the garden information to the public?

This does not necessarily have to be by means of a formal or expensive publication. All that is required is a one-page sheet that identifies the varieties of plants, whether they are heirlooms or not, and the rationale for their placement within the garden. Another resource is the list of garden history books in the selected bibliography.

Once these questions have been answered and your goals have been defined, use various archival materials to write a garden narrative that can be used to develop the landscape and interpretive plans. The Wisconsin Historical Society has an enormous collection of online images and newspaper articles. The landscape and garden photographs by Andreas Larsen Dahl, Charles Van Schaick, William Bass, and others available through the Wisconsin Historical Society's image library are an invaluable resource. Because they depict vernacular gardens as they actually existed—weeds and all—rather than carefully manicured landscapes meant for professional publications, they are the most accurate and genuine records available. Document your findings, being careful to cite your sources in detail. Use your research results to make an informed decision and knowledgeable evaluation about the form and composition of your vintage garden.

In terms of developing the landscape plan for your period garden or cultural landscape, an array of general literature is available to assist in your decision-making process. A very practical and helpful beginning is Charles Birnbaum's 1994 "Preservation Brief 36," published by the U.S. Department of the Interior, which provides background information on cultural landscape history. It also offers an overview and four specific guidelines for a formal approach to the landscape plan[5]:

> **1. Preservation.** This approach is defined as "the act or process of applying measures necessary to sustain the existing form, integrity, and materials of an historic property." There is little new construction and replacement of vegetation and/or buildings. This approach requires the least change.

The Belgian Farm at Heritage Hill State Historical Park accurately portrays the vegetable garden in the front of the house and close to the road as it would have looked in 1905.

JIM DOCKENDORFF

2. Rehabilitation. This is "the act or process of making possible a compatible use for a property through repair, alterations, and additions, while preserving those portions or features which convey its cultural or historic values." For example, a handrail might be added to a steep slope in a public garden for safety reasons. While not historically accurate, it may well be a legal requirement.

3. Restoration. Defined as "the act or process of accurately depicting the form, features, and character of a property as it appeared at a particular period of time," this type of renovation may include removal of specific features that were not in place during the determined interpretive time period. This approach may also require making difficult decisions regarding whether or not to remove post-interpretive-date hardscaping, buildings, or healthy trees.

4. Reconstruction. This process requires re-creating "the form, features, and detailing of a non-surviving site, landscape, building structure, or object for the purposes of replicating its appearance at a specific period of time." When historic buildings are relocated to sites such as Heritage Hill State Historical Park or Old World Wisconsin, their gardens, of course, must be reconstructed. Their appearance, however, is usually carefully researched to replicate, as much as is possible, the original landscape.

The ethnic farm gardens at Old World Wisconsin are an important feature of this outdoor living history site and accurately represent the varieties of plants available during the mid- to late nineteenth century. The re-created garden at the Schottler Farm represents the 1875 period of the home.
WISCONSIN HISTORICAL SOCIETY

The lack of primary documentation for the appearance of Heritage Hill State Historical Park's Tank Cottage garden in its interpretive year of 1871 was the main factor in the decision to reconstruct a generic urban garden of the era. The vegetable garden—with its picket fence, raised beds surrounded by crushed stone pathways, and mix of vegetable, herbs, and fruit bushes—illustrates the elements suggested by the Wisconsin State Horticultural Society for an 1870s urban garden.
JIM DOCKENDORFF

These formal approaches are used by the National Park Service to evaluate cultural landscape properties. Sometimes, however, a more informal approach combining aspects of all four treatment plans might better fit the landscape and its purpose. For example, the Old World Wisconsin historic homes and outbuildings were moved to their existing locations from other sites, necessitating complete reconstruction of their gardens; however, within the boundaries of the site are also several significant natural areas that are more appropriately treated with preservation, rehabilitation, or restoration plans. In general, these guidelines are a useful background tool when developing a landscape plan for a historic site, with the caveat that each site is unique and might benefit from a mix of approaches.

The historic gardens pictured here are invaluable resources for anyone who is interested in learning more about Wisconsin garden history or researching an individual home landscape. Each is unique, whether it represents the vegetable garden of a Belgian farm family or the large estate of a wealthy industrialist. Not all are vernacular, but each offers individual solutions to the challenges of heirloom gardening while providing visitors with a pleasurable and educational experience. There are other historic gardens in Wisconsin not pictured here and I hope that there will be more in the future. Though the rationale for developing a vintage garden may be based on the desire for historical accuracy, the benefits of such a garden are wide ranging. The delights of these gardens are multisensory: the aroma of antique roses, old-fashioned marigolds, or heirloom varieties of peonies; the flavor of an heirloom tomato or raspberry; and the vision of a diverse mass of colorful flowers against a trellis of deep green vines. Modern hybrids may have lengthier growing seasons, produce larger blossoms, and be more disease-resistant, but their fragrance and individuality has been lost. In a vintage garden, these can be reclaimed.

Women speakers at WSHS meetings were clearly well read and knowledgeable about their gardens and plants. Their voices, as well as those of their male colleagues, brought to life the dreams and aspirations they had for their gardens, their families, their communities, and their state. Through their writings, they unknowingly left a remarkable legacy that we can draw on today as an invaluable tool to help us understand how they created and enjoyed their gardens, and how to appreciate our own.

Today we may enjoy our gardens more for their sensory beauty than their spiritual and philosophical significance, but for these early Wisconsin citizens, the garden was a

Opposite page:
The Heritage Flower Farm in Mukwonago includes several acres with interconnecting gardens containing numerous varieties of field-grown perennials. Astilbe 'Fanal' is the standout here.
BETTY ADELMAN

Right: This tranquil and colorful summer meadow at Heritage Flower Farm features such native flowers as yarrow, liatris, coneflower, and joe-pye weed among others.
BETTY ADELMAN

Bottom right:
The Kneeland-Walker House & Gardens in Wauwatosa retains its 1920s layout with metal-edged curved beds.
CAROLYN DRESSLER,
WAUWATOSA HISTORICAL SOCIETY

Opposite page:
The small heritage garden at Crossroads at Big Creek was established by the Sturgeon Bay Garden Club to demonstrate the typical plants and vegetables grown in Door County around the turn of the twentieth century. Its arching entryway supports a vigorously climbing *Clematis tangutica*, a yellow, fall-blooming clematis once known as 'Russian Virgin's Bower.'
KATHERINE M. GREEN

metaphor for society. As Charlotte Lewis, the first female member of the WSHS, eloquently stated in 1874:

> *Let the honeysuckles, climbing roses, woodbine and morning glorys, come creeping everywhere; over the trees, balconies, fences, outbuildings and summer houses, to cheer and brighten our lives. . . .*
>
> *There is a sacred love of home planted in every human heart; let us cherish that love, and when we are beautifying our homes let us remember that it is not for our enjoyment alone. The tired laborer, the student, the traveler, the poor seamstress, the sick and wanderer, who have neither time, room, or means for such refinements, may find here cheer, courage, comfort, and long after will cherish the memory of its beauty, and it may awaken noble thoughts, impulses and resolutions, that will last for all time.*[6]

A page from the John A. Salzer Seed Company's 1919 catalog

Appendix: Recommended Varieties

The sources for these tables are the recommended varieties lists published by the Wisconsin State Horticultural Society between 1886 and 1928 in the *Transactions* and *Annual Reports*. These lists comprise many of the varieties recommended as being suitable for Wisconsin gardens. They by no means include the vast array of plants that were available during this time period.

Table 1: Evergreen trees

DATE FIRST LISTED	COMMON NAME	LATIN NAME	COMMENTS IN TEXT
1886	Balsam fir	*Abies balsamea*	
1886	Norway spruce	*Picea excelsa*	large
1886	Austrian pine	*Pinus austriaca*	large
1886	Red pine	*Pinus resinous*	large
1886	White pine	*Pinus strobus*	large
1886	Scotch pine	*Pinus sylvestris*	large
1886	Arbor Vitae (white cedar)	*Thuja occidentalis*	large
1886	Siberian Arbor Vitae	*Thuja orientalis,* var.	
1886	Hemlock spruce	*Tsuga canadensis*	large
1894	Red cedar	*Juniperus virginiana*	
1896	Juniper	*Juniperus sabina*	
1896	Pyramidal Arbor Vitae	*Thuja pyramidalis*	
1904	Sabin juniper	*Juniperus sabina*	
1904	White spruce	*Picea canadensis*	large
1904	Mugho pine	*Pinus montana,* var. *Mughus*	
1905	Colorado blue spruce	*Picea pungeons*	large
1920	Concolor fir	*Abies concolor*	large
1920	Waukegan juniper	*Juniperus horizontalis*	
1920	Dwarf juniper	*Juniperus communis,* var.	

Table 1: Evergreen trees (continued)

DATE FIRST LISTED	COMMON NAME	LATIN NAME	COMMENTS IN TEXT
1920	Japanese trailing juniper	*Juniperus procumbens*	
1920	Tamarix-leaved juniper	*Juniperus sabina*, var.	
1920	Bull pine	*Pinus ponderosa*	large
1920	Douglas fir	*Pseudotsuga taxifolia*	large
1920	American yew	*Taxus cadanensis*	
1921	Globe arborvitae	*Thuja compacta*	

Table 2: Deciduous trees

DATE FIRST LISTED	COMMON NAME	LATIN NAME	COMMENTS IN TEXT
1886	Mountain ash (native)	*Pyrus americana*	small ornamental
1886	American elm	*Ulmus americana*	street planting
1886	American larch	*Larix laricina*	"timber" tree
1886	Basswood	*Tilia americana*	street planting
1886	Black cherry	*Prunus serontina*	"timber" tree
1886	Black walnut	*Juglans nigra*	"timber" tree
1886	Box elder, ash-leaved maple	*Acer negundo*	"timber" tree
1886	European larch	*Larix europea*	"timber" tree
1886	Green ash	*Fraxinus viridis aesculus*	"timber" tree
1886	Horse-chestnut	*Hippocastanum*	
1886	Norway maple	*Acer plantinoides*	street planting
1886	Paper birch	*Betula papyrifera*	also named canoe birch
1886	Weeping poplar		
1886	White ash	*Fraxinus americana*	"timber" tree
1886	White oak	*Quercus alba*	
1886	Wisconsin weeping willow	*Salix babylonica*, var.	an exotic, introduced in 1730
1893	Kentucky coffee tree	*Gymnocladus canadensis*	
1897	Laurel willow	*Salix pentandra*, var. of *Salix babylonica*	
1904	Carolina poplar	*Populus monilifera gleditschea*	
1904	Honey locust	*Triacanthos*	

DATE FIRST LISTED	COMMON NAME	LATIN NAME	COMMENTS IN TEXT
1904	Red oak	*Quercus coccinea*	
1904	Russian mulberry	*Morus alba*, var. *Tartarica*	
1904	Silver maple	*Acer dasycarpum*	
1904	Sugar maple	*Acer saccharinum*	
1904	Tartarian maple	*Acer tartaricum*	small ornamental
1905	Scarlet maple	*Acer rubrum*	
1915	Bechtel's double-flowering crab	*Pyrus*, var. *Bechtellii*	small ornamental
1915	Western crab apple (native)	*Pyrus ioensis*	small ornamental
1920	Bolles poplar	*Populus bolleana*	
1920	Buckeye	*Aesculus glabra*	
1920	Burr oak	*Quercus macrocarpa*	
1920	Golden willow	*Salix vitellina,* var. of *Salix babylonica*	
1920	Hackberry	*Celtis occidentalis*	
1920	Hawthorn	*Crataegus crus-galli*	small ornamental
1920	Ironwood	*Ostrya virginiana amelanchier*	
1920	Juneberry	*Canadensis*	
1920	Maidenhair tree	*Ginko biloba*	
1920	Pin oak	*Quercus palustria*	street planting
1920	Red oak	*Quercus rubra*	
1920	Wiers cut leaf maple	*Acer dasycarpum*, var.	

Table 3a: Shrubs listed before 1904

DATE FIRST LISTED	COMMON NAME	LATIN NAME
1886	Thunberg's barberry	*Berberis thunbergii*
1886	Purple-leaved barberry	*Berberis vulgaris*
1886	Purple filbert	*Corylus maxima*
1886	Smoke tree	*Cotinus coggyria*
1886	Winged burning bush	*Euonymus alata*
1886	Wahoo, burning bush, American strawberry tree	*Euonymus atropupurus*
1886	Summer snowball, hardy hydrangea	*Hydrangea arborescens*
1886	Ruprecht's honeysuckle	*Lonicera ruprechtiana*
1886	Shrubby cinquefoil	*Potentilla fructicosa*
1886	Golden elder	*Sambucus nigra*, var. *aurea*
1886	Spirea	*Spirea, Prunifolia* and others
1886	Downy lilac	*Syringa villosa*
1886	Common lilac	*Syringa vulgaris*
1886	Wayfaring tree	*Viburnum lantana*
1886	Snowball	*Viburnum opulus*, var. *sterile*
1886	Highbush cranberry	*Viburnum trilobum*
1894	Mountain maple	*Acer spicatum*
1894	Flowering quince	*Chaenomoles*
1894	Deutzia	*Deutzia gracales*
1894	Weigela	*Diervilla florida*
1894	Hydrangea	*Hydrangea grandiflora*
1897	Russian almond	*Prunus nana*

Table 3b: Shrubs listed after 1904

DATE FIRST LISTED	COMMON NAME	LATIN NAME
1904	Weigela, 'Eva Rathke'	*Diervilla hybrida*
1904	Silver berry	*Eleagnus argenta*
1904	Garden hydrangea	*Hydrangea paniculata*
1904	Morrow's honeysuckle	*Lonicera morrowi*
1904	Mock orange, large	*Philadelphus inodorus*
1905	Philadelphia dogwood	*Cornus philadelphus*
1905	Strawberry tree	*Euonymus europaeus*
1905	Amur privet	*Ligustrum amurense*
1905	Upright honeysuckle	*Lonicera tatarica*
1905	Tea's weeping mulberry	*Morus alba*
1905	Mock orange	*Philadelphus coronarius*
1905	Lemoine's Philadelphus	*Philadelphus lemoinii*
1905	Dwarf flowering almond	*Prunus gladiolus*
1905	Buckthorn	*Rhamnus*
1905	Smoke bush	*Rhus cotinus*
1905	Alpine currant	*Ribes alpinum*
1905	Missouri flowering currant	*Ribes aurium*
1905	Rose acacia	*Robinia hispida*
1905	Japanese rose	*Rosa rugosa*
1905	Cut leaf elder	*Sambucus canadensis*, var. *acutiloba*
1905	Buffalo berry	*Shepherdia argenta*
1905	Billard's spirea	*Spirea billardii*
1905	Callosa spirea	*Spirea callosa*, *alba* and *rubra*
1905	Bridal wreath	*Spirea prunifolia*
1905	Persian lilac	*Syringa persica*
1920	Forsythia	*Forsythia intermedia*
1920	Regal's privet	*Ligustrum ibota*, var.
1920	Cut leaf sumac	*Rhus typhina* and *glabra*

Table 4: "Black list"

COMMON NAME	LATIN NAME	COMMON NAME	LATIN NAME
Arguta spirea	*Spirea arguta*	Kerria	*Kerria japonica*
Azalea	*Azalea nudiflora*	Paulownia	*Paulownia imperialis*
Azalea	*Azalea mollis*	Pearl bush	*Exocorda grandiflora*
Bladder senna	*Colutea arborescens*	Purple-leaved plum	*Prunus cerasifera*
Blue spirea	*Caryoteris mastacanthus*	Rhododendron	*Azalea arborescens*
Common privet	*Ligustrum vulgare*	Rhododendron	*Azalea viscosa*
Daphne	*Daphne cneorum*	Slender deutzia	*Deutzia gracilis*
Daphne	*Daphne mezercum*	Snowdrop tree	*Halesia tetraptera*
Flowering almond	*Prunus japonica*	Sweet pepperbush	*Clethra alnifolia*
Flowering dogwood	*Cornus florida*	Sweet-scented shrub	*Calycanthus floridus*
Flowering plum (double)	*Prunus triloba*	Thunberg's spirea	*Spirea thunbergii*
Golden bell	*Forsythia suspensa*	Virginia willow	*Itea virginica*
Goumi	*Elaeagnus longipes*	White fringe	*Chionanthus virginica*
Japanese quince	*Cydonia japonica*		

Annual Reports, 1906–1919. After 1919, the name of the list was amended to read "Plants needing winter protection."

Table 5: Native shrubs recommended after 1906

COMMON NAME	LATIN NAME	COMMON NAME	LATIN NAME
Bearberry	*Arctostaphylus uva-ursi*	Winterberry (ivy)	*Ilex verticillata*
New Jersey tea	*Ceanothos americanus*	Trailing juniper	*Juniperus procumbens*
Button bush	*Cephalanthus occidentalis*	Sweet gale	*Myrica gale*
Princes' pine	*Cimaphila umbellata*	Ninebark	*Physocarpos opulifolia*
Round-leaved dogwood	*Comptonia aspleniflora*	Buckthorn	*Rhamnus catharticus*
Red Osier dogwood	*Cornus stolinifera*	Staghorn sumac	*Rhus typhina*
Leatherwood (wickopy)	*Dirca palustris*	Smooth sumac	*Rhus glabra*
Trailing arbutus	*Epigaea repens*	Dwarf sumac	*Rhus copalina*
Wahoo	*Euonymous atropurpureus*	Wild red currant	*Ribes rubrum*
St. John's wort	*Hypericum pyramidatum*	Wild black currant	*Ribes floridum*

COMMON NAME	LATIN NAME	COMMON NAME	LATIN NAME
Wild rose (tall)	*Rosa lucida*	Coralberry	*Symphoricarpus vulgaris*
Wild rose (short)	*Rosa blanda*	Ground hemlock	*Taxus baccata*
Purple-flowered raspberry	*Rubus odaratus*	Sheepberry	*Viburnun lentago*
White-flowered raspberry	*Rubus nutkanus*	Black haw	*Viburnum dentatum*
Common elder	*Sambucus canadensis*	no name given	*Viburnum acerifolium*
Scarlet elder	*Sambucus pubens*	Bush cranberry	*Viburnum opulus*
Snowberry	*Symphoricarpus racemosus*	Prickly ash	*Zantoxylum americanum*

Table 6: Perennials recommended after 1915

COMMON NAME	LATIN AND OTHER NAMES	COMMON NAME	LATIN AND OTHER NAMES
Milfoil	*Achillea ptarmica*, 'The Pearl'	Tiger lily	*Lilium tigrinum*
		Garden lily	*Lilium elegans*
Columbine	*Aquilegia*, long-spurred hybrid and many varieties	Garden lily	*Lilium dauricum*
		Oriental poppy	*Papaver orientale*
False chamomile	*Boltonia asteroides* and *latisquama*	Peony	*Peony*, many varieties
		Peony	*Rubra superba*, late red
Canterbury bells	*Campanula carpatica*	Peony	'Felix Crousse', midseason red
Peach bells	*Campanula persicaefolia*		
Shasta daisy	*Chrysanthemum maximum*	Peony	'Marie Lemoine', late white
Tickseed	*Coreopsis lanceolata*		
Larkspur	*Delphinium, Belladonna*, and *Formosum*, hybrids	Peony	*Festiva maxima*, early white
		Peony	'Mad. Emile Gauille', shell pink
Grass pink	*Dianthus plumarius*		
Blanket flower	*Gaillardia grandiflora*	Peony	*Edulis superba*, early pink
Baby's breath	*Gypsophilia paniculata*	Phlox	*Phlox*, many varieties
Day lily	*Hemoracallis*, several varieties	Phlox	'Elizabeth Campbell', light salmon pink
Fleur-de-lis	*Iris*, scores of varieties *Mad. Chereau Honorabilia*	Phlox	*Europea, white*, carmine eye
Artemesia	'Silver King' 'Queen of May' 'Pallida Damatica'	Phlox	'Mrs. Jenkins', white
		Phlox	'B. compte', French purple
Blue poppy	*Papaver orientalis*, blue	Phlox	'R. P. Struthers', bright rosy red

Table 6: Perennials recommended after 1915 (continued)

COMMON NAME	LATIN AND OTHER NAMES	COMMON NAME	LATIN AND OTHER NAMES
Phlox	'Beranger', delicate pink	Purple cone flower	*Rudbeckia purpurea*
Phlox	'Miss Lingard', early white, pink eye	Stonecrop	*Sedum spectabilis*
Balloon flower	*Platycodon grandiflora*	Speedwell	*Veronica spicata*
Giant daisy	*Pyrethrum ulligonosum*		
Persian daisy	*Pyrethrum roseum*		

Annual Reports, 1915–1928

Table 7: Native perennials recommended for the home garden in 1915

COMMON NAME	LATIN NAME	COMMON NAME	LATIN NAME
New England aster	*Aster novae anglae*	Turk's cap lily	*Lilium superbum*
Prairie anemone	*Anemone pennsylvanica*	Cardinal lobelia	*Lobelia cardinalis*
Badger or pasque flower	*Anemone pulsatilla*	Lungwort	*Mertensia virginica*
Butterfly weed	*Asclepias tuberosa*	Woods phlox	*Phlox divaricata*
Columbine	*Aquilegia canadensis*	Prairie phlox	*Phlox pilosia*
Harebell	*Campanula rotundifolia*	False dragonhead	*Physostegia virginica*
Shooting star	*Dodocatheon media*	Greek valerian	*Polemonium reptans*
White snakeroot	*Eupatorium ageratoides*	Black-eyed Susan	*Rudbeckia hirta*
Flowering spurge	*Euphorbica corollata*	Spider lily	*Tradescantia virginica*
Sneezewort	*Helenium autumnale*	White Wake robin	*Trillium grandiflorum*
Blazing star	*Liatris squarrosa*	Speedwell	*Veronica virginica*
Native lily	*Lilium canadense*	Bird's-foot violet	*Viola pedata*

Annual Reports, 1915–1928

Table 8: Recommended vines

DATE FIRST LISTED	COMMON NAME	LATIN NAME
1886	Virginia creeper, *Ampelopsis*	*Ampelopsis quinquefolia*
1886	Climbing bittersweet	*Celastrus scandens*
1886	Jackmanii clematis	*Clematis jackmanii*
1886	Virgin's bower, native clematis	*Clematis virginiana*
1886	Fragrant honeysuckle Trumpet honeysuckle Scarlet honeysuckle	*Lonicera caprifolium* *Lonicera semperverens*
1915	Grape ivy	*Vitis riparia ampeolpsis quinquefolia*, var.
1920	Engleman's ivy	*Englemanii*
1920	Japanese clematis	*Clematis paniculata*
1920	Wild grape	*Vitis labrusca*

Table 9: Recommended roses

DATE FIRST LISTED	CULTIVAR	CLASS
1886	'General Jacqeminot'	hybrid perpetual
1886	'General Washington'	hybrid perpetual
1886	'Harrison's Yellow'	hybrid perpetual
1886	'Luxembourg'	moss
1886	'Persian'	briar
1886	'Princess Adelaide'	hybrid perpetual
1886	'Queen of the Prairie'	climber
1886	'Salet'	moss
1893	'Deuil de Paul Fontaine'	moss
1893	'Henri Martin'	hybrid perpetual
1893	'Madame Plantier'	hybrid perpetual
1893	'Magna Charta'	hybrid perpetual
1893	'Marshall P. Wilder'	hybrid perpetual
1893	'Mrs. John Lainge'	hybrid perpetual
1893	'Paul Neyron'	hybrid perpetual
1893	'Prince Camille de Rohan'	hybrid perpetual

Table 9: Recommended roses (continued)

DATE FIRST LISTED	CULTIVAR	CLASS
1893	'Vick's Caprice'	hybrid perpetual
1894	'American Beauty'	hybrid perpetual
1894	'Coquette des Blanches'	hybrid perpetual
1894	Cottage	climber
1894	'Dinsmore'	hybrid perpetual
1894	'Earl of Dufferin'	hybrid perpetual
1894	'Gem of the Prairies'	climber
1894	'Jules Margottin'	hybrid perpetual
1894	'Perpetual White'	moss
1894	'Seven Sisters'	climber
1894	'Victor Verdier'	climber
1897	'Crimson Rambler'	climber
1915	'Dorothy Perkins'	climber
1920	'Captain Christy'	hybrid perpetual
1920	'Conrad F. Meyer'	hardy garden
1920	'Crested Moss'	moss
1920	Druschki ('Frau Karl Druschki')	hybrid perpetual
1920	'Excelsa'	climber
1920	'John Hopper'	hybrid perpetual
1920	Rosa rugosa	hardy garden
1920	'Ulrich Brunner'	hybrid perpetual
1925	'American Pillar'	climber
1925	'Baron de Bonstetten'	hybrid perpetual
1925	'Cabbage Rose'	hardy garden

Notes

Foreword

1. Annette Kolodny, *The Land Before Her: Fantasy and Experience of the American Frontiers, 1630–1860* (Chapel Hill: University of North Carolina Press, 1984), xiii.

2. Mrs. D. Huntley, "Rural Homes," *Transactions of the Wisconsin State Horticultural Society* (1873), 160; the quotation may be found on page 43 of this book.

Introduction

1. Membership distribution and ethnicity are discussed in chapter 3.

2. Complete copies of these publications are located at the Wisconsin Historical Society and Steenbock Memorial libraries on the University of Wisconsin–Madison campus. The *Transactions of the Wisconsin State Horticultural Society*, *Annual Reports of the Wisconsin State Horticultural Society*, *The Wisconsin Horticulturist*, and *Wisconsin Horticulture* are also available in electronic form at http://digital.library.wisc.edu/1711.dl/WI. To access these reports, scroll down to "Materials in the Collection" and click on "A History of Wisconsin Agriculture and Rural Life." Click on "Browse the History of Wisconsin Agriculture and Rural Life Collection" and then scroll down to Wisconsin State Horticultural Society publications, near the bottom of the list. But beware of getting sidetracked in the staggering array of subjects!

3. Membership lists of annual, life, and honorary members were published annually in WSHS reports between 1869 and 1900, and occasionally thereafter.

Chapter 1

1. Andrew Jackson Downing, *Cottage Residences; or, A Series of Designs for Rural Cottages and Cottage Villas and Their Gardens and Grounds. Adapted to North America*, 3rd ed. (New York: Wiley and Putnam, 1847), ix.

2. Anne Scott-James, *The Cottage Garden* (Middlesex, England: Penguin Books, 1981), 9–12.

3. Ann Leighton, *Early American Gardens: "For Meate and Medicine"* (Boston: Houghton Mifflin, 1970). Leighton uses this quotation as a subtitle in her trilogy of American garden history. She attributes it to seventeenth-century English physician John Parkinson.

4. Diane Kostial McGuire, "Early Gardens Along the Atlantic Coast," in *Keeping Eden: A History of Gardening in America*, ed. Walter Punch (Boston: Little, Brown and Company, 1992), 14.

5. Ibid., 25.

6. Ibid., 26.

7. Charles E. Beveridge, "Frederick Law Olmsted," in *American Landscape Architecture: Designers and Places*, ed. William H. Tishler (Washington, DC: The Preservation Press, 1989), 38.

PAINTED FOR VICK'S MONTHLY.

SMALL FLOWERED PETUNIAS.

Lithographic & Chromo Co. of Rochester N.Y.

Opposite page:
Petunias

VICK'S MONTHLY MAGAZINE,
MAY 1879

8. Jacob Weidenmann, *Beautifying Country Homes* (New York: Orange Judd and Company, 1870).

9. Denise Wiles Adams, *Restoring American Gardens: An Encyclopedia of Heirloom Ornamental Plants, 1640–1940* (Portland: Timber Press, 2004), 208.

10. Fred E. H. Schroeder, *Front Yard America: The Evolution and Meaning of a Vernacular Domestic Landscape* (Bowling Green, OH: Bowling Green State University Press, 1993), 80–96.

11. Frank J. Scott, *The Art of Beautifying Suburban Home Grounds of Small Extent: The Advantage of Suburban Homes over City or Country Homes; The Comfort and Economy of Neighboring Improvements; The Choice and Treatment of Building Sites; and the Best Modes of Laying Out, Planting and Keeping Decorated Grounds* (New York: Appleton & Co., 1870), 121, 129.

12. H. W. S. Cleveland, *Landscape Architecture, As Applied to the Wants of the West* (Chicago: Jansen, McClurg & Co., 1873), preface.

13. Ibid., 17. The current American Society of Landscape Architects definition of the term is that landscape architecture "encompasses the analysis, planning, design, management, and stewardship of the natural and built environments," http://www.asla.org.

14. Ibid., 81.

15. Ibid., 18–27.

16. William H. Tishler, "H. W. S. Cleveland," in *American Landscape Architecture: Designers and Places* (Washington, DC: The Preservation Press, 1989), 27.

17. Cleveland, *Landscape Architecture*, 13.

18. Ibid., 13.

19. Warren H. Manning, *A Handbook for Planning and Planting Small Home Grounds* (Menomonie, WI: Stout Manual Training School, 1899).

20. Manning's suggestions are discussed in more detail in chapter 5.

21. Wilhelm Miller, *The Prairie Spirit in Landscape Gardening*, Circular Number 184 (Urbana: University of Illinois Agricultural Experiment Station, 1915), 18.

22. O. C. Simonds, *Landscape-Gardening* (New York: The MacMillan Company, 1920), 8–19.

23. University of Wisconsin–Madison, Department of Landscape Architecture, "History of the Program," http://www.la.wisc.edu/history/index.htm.

24. Mrs. Laura Smith, "Floriculture," *Transactions of the Wisconsin State Agricultural Society* 3 (1853), 257.

25. Joseph Breck, *The Flower-Garden; Or, Breck's Book of Flowers; in Which are Described All the Various Hardy Herbaceous Perennials, Annuals, Shrubby Plants, and Evergreen Trees, Desirable for Ornamental Purposes, With Directions for their Cultivation* (Boston: John P. Jewitt & Co., 1851), 18.

26. The lawn mower had been invented in 1830 by Englishman Edwin Budding; it was not imported into America until 1855. D. Keith Crotz, "Science and Technology in the American Garden," in *Keeping Eden: A History of Gardening in America*, ed. Walter Punch (Boston: Little, Brown and Company, 1992), 138.

27. Patricia Tice, "Gardens of Change," in *American Home Life, 1880–1930: A Social History of Space and Services*, ed. Jessica H. Foy and Thomas J. Schlereth (Knoxville: University of Tennessee Press, 1992), 196.

28. Gertrude Jekyll, *Color Schemes for the Flower Garden* (London: Country Life Ltd., 1908), iv.

29. Its significance to the Wisconsin vernacular gardens will be discussed in more detail in chapter 5.

30. Liberty Hyde Bailey, *Manual of Gardening; A Practical Guide to the Making of Home Grounds and the Growing of Flowers, Fruits, and Vegetables for Home Use* (Norwood, MA: Norwood Press, 1910), 2.

31. Ibid., 3.

32. Robert Grese, "Bailey, Liberty Hyde," in *Pioneers of American Landscape Design: An Annotated Bibliography*, ed. Charles Birnbaum and Lisa Crowder (Washington, DC: National Park Service, 1993), 9–11.

33. James Vick, "Publisher's Note," in *Home Floriculture: A Familiar Guide to the Treatment of Flowering and Other Ornamental Plants in the House and Garden*, ed. Eben Rexford (Rochester, NY: James Vick, 1890), ix.

34. This work is cited by virtually all American garden historians, including Leighton, Adams, and Tice.

35. Mary E. Smith, *Eben E. Rexford: A Biographical Sketch; a Memorial Containing "Silver Threads Among the Gold" and His Last Poem* (Philadelphia: Lippincott, 1917), 34. Rexford wrote the lyrics for the enormously popular song "Silver Threads Among the Gold," as well as numerous hymns.

36. Rexford published a photographic essay of a trip he took to northern Wisconsin, using photographs that he took himself. His biography suggests that he used his own garden for experimentation with the growing habits and patterns of plants.

37. Rexford, *Home Floriculture*, 213.

38. Zona Gale, "Civic Improvement in the Little Towns" (Washington, DC: American Civic Association, 1913), 3.

39. Gustav Stickley, *Craftsman Homes* (New York: The Craftsman Publishing Company, 1909), 1.

40. Tice, "Gardens of Change," 191–207.

41. Louisa Yeomans King, "Editor's Preface," in *Design in the Little Garden*, by Fletcher Steele (Boston: Atlantic Monthly Press, 1924), v.

42. Ibid.

43. Steele, *Design in the Little Garden*, 31.

44. Ibid., 46.

45. Grace Tabor, *The Landscape Gardening Book* (Philadelphia: The John C. Winston Company, 1911), 120.

46. Steele, *Design in the Little Garden*, 42.

Chapter 2

1. Mrs. Ida Tilson, "Looking Backward in Wisconsin," *Annual Report of the Wisconsin State Horticultural Society* 21 (1891), 188.

2. Michael Gallagher and Amelia Janes, "Glacial Landscapes," in *Wisconsin's Past and Present: A Historical Atlas*, ed. Wisconsin Cartographer's Guild (Madison: University of Wisconsin Press, 2002), 32.

3. Amelia Janes, "Early Cultures," in *Wisconsin's Past and Present: A Historical Atlas*, ed. Wisconsin Cartographer's Guild (Madison: University of Wisconsin Press, 2002), 2–3.

4. Interpretive Staff of Heritage Hill State Historical Park, "Fort Howard Interpretive Plan" (Green Bay, WI: Heritage Hill State Historical Park, 1980, 1990), on file in the Heritage Hill State Historical Park Archives.

5. Ibid., n.p.

6. Robert C. Ostergren, "The Euro-American Settlement of Wisconsin, 1830–1920," in *Wisconsin Land and Life*, ed. Robert C. Ostergren and Thomas R. Vale (Madison: University of Wisconsin Press, 1997), 139.

7. Jeffry Maas, "Population and Representation," in *Wisconsin's Past and Present: A Historical Atlas*, ed. Wisconsin Cartographer's Guild (Madison: University of Wisconsin Press, 2002), 82.

8. Sharon D. Crawford, "The Development and Evolution of Domestic Gardens in Southern Wisconsin During the Nineteenth Century" (master's thesis, Department of Landscape Architecture, University of Wisconsin–Madison, 1983), 21.

9. Ostergren, "The Euro-American Settlement of Wisconsin," 142.

10. Clarence W. Olmstead, "Changing Technology, Values, and Rural Landscapes," in *Wisconsin Land and Life*, ed. Robert C. Ostergren and Thomas R. Vale (Madison: University of Wisconsin Press, 1997), 362.

11. Ibid.

12. Keith N. Morgan, "Garden and Forest: Nineteenth-Century Development in Landscape Architecture," in *Keeping Eden: A History of Gardening in America*, ed. Walter Punch (Boston: Little, Brown and Company, 1992), 32.

13. "Constitution of the Wisconsin State Agricultural Society," *Transactions of the Wisconsin State Agricultural Society* 1 (1851), 1.

14. Crawford, "Domestic Gardens in Southern Wisconsin," 40.

15. Ibid., 160.

16. Ibid.

17. Ibid.

18. Ibid.

19. Ibid., 78.

20. Ibid., 67.

21. Mrs. Laura Smith, "Floriculture," *Transactions of the Wisconsin State Agricultural Society* 3 (1853), 254.

22. Crawford, "Domestic Gardens in Southern Wisconsin," 164.

23. Ibid.

24. Ibid., 165.

25. Ibid., 168.

26. Olmstead, "Changing Technology, Values, and Rural Landscapes," 360–365.

27. Ibid., 362.

28. Gallagher, "Becoming German-American," 18. Until 1871, modern-day Germany consisted of a number of independent states, including Pomerania, Bavaria, and Prussia.

29. James William Miller, "German Heirloom Gardening Research Report," 2002. Unpublished document, on file in the archives at Old World Wisconsin, Eagle, Wisconsin.

30. Miller, "German Heirloom Gardening," 43–68.

31. Crawford, "Domestic Gardens in Southern Wisconsin," 77.

32. Ostergren, "The Euro-American Settlement of Wisconsin," 143.

33. Joseph Schafer, *A History of Agriculture in Wisconsin* (Madison: State Historical Society of Wisconsin, 1922), 165.

34. Mark Speltz, "An Interest in Health and Happiness as Yet Untold: The Woman's Club of Madison, 1893–1917," *Wisconsin Magazine of History* 89, no. 3 (Spring 2006), 5.

35. Ibid, 10.

Chapter 3

1. Mrs. D. Huntley, "Rural Homes," *Transactions of the Wisconsin State Horticultural Society* (1873), 160.

2. Henry J. Rahmlow, *A History of Seventy-Five Years of Service by the Wisconsin State Horticultural Society* (Madison: Wisconsin State Horticultural Society, 1943), 8.

3. Frederic Cranefield, "Constitution and By-Laws of the Wisconsin State Horticultural Society, with a brief historical outline," *Combined Annual Reports of the Wisconsin State Horticultural Society for the Years Ending July 1, 1927 and July 1, 1928* 57, vii.

4. As an example, the following names appeared in the 1910 membership list: Ernest Gonzenbach, Sheboygan; Henry Naffz, Sauk City; and A. L. Kreutzer, Wausau. *Annual Report of the Wisconsin State Horticultural Society* 40, part 1 (1910), 13–24.

5. "Membership Roll," *Annual Report* 40, part 1 (1910), 25–31.

6. The contribution of the WSHS to the development of the apple industry in Wisconsin has been well documented by Cortney Cain in "The Development of Apple Horticulture in Wisconsin, 1850s–1860s: Case Studies of Bayfield, Crawford, and Door Counties" (master's thesis, Department of Landscape Architecture, University of Wisconsin–Madison, 2006).

7. The contents of these presentations are addressed in detail in chapters 5 and 6.

8. Tamara Plakins Thornton, "Horticulture and American Character," in *Keeping Eden: A History of Gardening in America* (Boston: Massachusetts Horticultural Society, 1992), 199.

9. H. W. Roby, "Pleasures and Benefits of Amateur Florticulture," *Transactions* (1871), 89.

10. Henry T. Williams, "Rural Taste," *Transactions* (1872), 174.

11. The first two female members were Charlotte Lewis (her articles are listed with her husband's initials: "Mrs. H. M. Lewis") of Madison and Mrs. Vie H. Campbell of Evansville.

12. "Discussion," *Transactions* 14 (1884), 107.

13. Mrs. Prof. A. Kerr, "Woman in the Garden," *Transactions* 10 (1880), 236.

14. Vie H. Campbell, "Announcement," *The Wisconsin Horticulturist* 1, no. 12 (February 1897), 31–33.

15. Frederic Cranefield, "Annual Report," *Annual Report* 57 ([1928?]), 20.

16. O. C. Simmons, "Planting a School Ground," *Transactions* 16 (1886), 271–274.

17. "Arbor Day Celebration," *Annual Report* 21 (1891), 214.

18. Ibid.

19. "Discussion," *Annual Report* 22 (1892), 171.

20. Prof. E. S. Goff, "Village Improvement, Societies and Arbor Day," *Annual Report* 22 (1892), 165–171.

21. "Society Membership Going Up," *Wisconsin Horticulture* 20, no. 2 (October 1930), 44.

22. "Plant a Victory Garden," in "Helpful Hints for the Beginner in Gardening and Fruit Growing," supplement, *Wisconsin Horticulture* 9, no. 6 (February 1919), 3–12; Wisconsin Gardeners, *The Wisconsin Garden Book* (Madison: Wisconsin State Horticultural Society, 1922).

23. The announcement states in full: "'City and Home Adornment Can Wait.' Governor Philipp says in his message to you: 'I wish to again impress upon the people of this state that the food situation is so serious that we will commit a moral wrong against our government if we in any way unnecessarily interfere with the production and successful harvesting of our agricultural products.

"Any community which now expends time and money purely for adornment is committing 'a moral wrong against our government.' These things can wait. Use this energy and money to get gardens planted. The individual, no matter how comfortable he may be financially who now spends large sums in beautifying his home grounds and nothing in the effort to increase the production of food is committing 'a moral wrong against our government.' Keep up the parks, but spend nothing additional on them. Keep your home grounds neat and attractive but plant more potatoes and fewer flowers,—this year. Next year we can make up for lost time." *Wisconsin Horticulture*, 7, special edition (April 17, 1917), 4.

24. "'Pro' Fruit Men Oust Cranefield Because He Wanted to Help Amateurs," *Capital Times*, November 15, 1926.

25. The Wisconsin Garden Club Federation remains an active organization and publishes a quarterly magazine, *Wisconsin Gardens*; http://www.wisconsingardenclub.org.

26. Henry Rahmlow and the Wisconsin Apple and Horticultural Society, *One Hundred Years: The Wisconsin State Horticultural Society, 1868–1968* (Madison: Wisconsin Apple and Horticultural Council, 1968), 55.

27. "Annual Meeting: Annual Address," *Report of the Wisconsin State Horticultural Society for the year 1869* (1870), 12–13.

28. Frederic Cranefield, "The Improvement of Home Grounds," *Annual Report* 34 (1904), 264.

29. "Design in the Garden," *Wisconsin Horticulture* 20, no. 7 (March 1930), 198.

30. Frances Kinsley Hutchinson, *Our Country Home: How We Transformed a Wisconsin Woodland* (Chicago: A. C. McClurg & Co., 1907). After Frances Hutchinson's death in 1935, the estate was deeded to the University of Chicago, which operated it as a nature preserve for several years before selling it. Neither the house nor grounds are extant.

Chapter 4

1. Dr. H. Allen, "Garden Floriculture," *Transactions of the Wisconsin State Horticultural Society* 10 (1880), 335–336.

2. The majority of the presentations consisted of recommendations for varieties of trees, shrubs, flowers, and vegetables suitable for home planting. These were incorporated into the annual WSHS recommended varieties lists and are discussed in chapter 5.

3. Frederic Cranefield, "The Improvement of Home Grounds," *Annual Report of the Wisconsin State Horticultural Society* 34 (1904), 264–302.

4. This may have been Cranefield's own decision: as secretary of the WSHS and editor of *Wisconsin Horticulture*, he was influential in the choice of agenda and journal contents.

5. Thomas Hislop, "Laying Out Grounds, Floriculture, Etc.," *Transactions of the Wisconsin State Agricultural Society* 2 (1852), 436.

Painted For Vicks Monthly
GARDEN VASE.

6. Charles Ramsdell, "Planning and Planting Home Grounds," *Annual Report* 30 (1900), 218.

7. H. W. S. Cleveland, *Landscape Architecture, As Applied to the Wants of the West* (Chicago: Jansen, McClurg & Co., 1873), 21.

8. Ibid.

9. Prof. Beale, "Ornamental Planting," *Transactions* 15 (1885), 158.

10. Prof. E. S. Goff, "The Adornment of Home Grounds," *Transactions* 21 (1891), 35.

11. Announcement by Charles H. Ramsdell. "A Handbook for Planning and Planting Home Grounds" *The Wisconsin Horticulturist* 5, no. 8 (October 1900), 32. It leads with: "A handbook valuable both to the horticulturist and amateur home gardener has lately been issued by the Stout Manual Training school of Menomonie. It was published for direct use with the collection of desirable natives and hardy exotics on the school grounds. But it also contains much useful information to any one interested in plants. It is written by Warren H. Manning of Boston, the well known landscape architect, who is in charge of the development of the collection. Therefore it is an authority in its own field of outdoor work."

12. Warren H. Manning, *A Handbook for Planning and Planting Small Home Grounds* (Menomonie, WI: Stout Manual Training School, 1899), 6–7.

13. Ramsdell, "Planning and Planting Home Grounds," 217.

14. F. C. Edwards, "Lawn Decoration," *Annual Report* 31 (1901), 246.

15. Delbert Utter, "Home Grounds," *Annual Report* 33 (1903), 207, 210.

16. E. H. Niles, "Planting the Home Grounds," *Wisconsin Horticulture* 4, no. 6 (February 1914), 3.

17. Ibid., 2.

18. Prof. C. E. Carey, "Flighty Vistas About the Home Grounds," *Annual Report* 56 (1926), 35.

19. E. A. Petranek, "It's Not a Home Until It's Planted" pts. 1, 2, and 3, *Wisconsin Horticulture* 18, no. 7 (March 1928), 157–159; no. 8 (April 1928), 192–193.

20. "Design in the Garden," *Wisconsin Horticulture* 20, no. 7 (March 1930), 197.

21. Ibid., 197–198.

22. Alfred L. Boerner, "Landscaping an English Home," *Wisconsin Horticulture* 20, no. 7 (March 1930), 205. Boerner, who served as the Milwaukee County Landscape Architect from 1926 to 1955, designed the first five formal gardens at the botanical garden that now bears his name; http://www.boernerbotanicalgardens.org.

23. Thomas Hislop, "Laying Out Grounds, Floriculture, Etc.," 438.

24. Ibid.

25. "Effect of a Good Fence," *The Wisconsin Horticulturist* 3, no. 3 (May 1898), 17.

26. Cranefield, "The Improvement of Home Grounds," 289, 297.

27. Ibid., 295.

28. Mrs. Vie H. Campbell, "The Farmer's Necessities," *Transactions* 15 (1885), 61.

29. Mrs. D. Huntley, "The Farmer's Dooryard," *Transactions* 10 (1880), 63.

30. F. C. Edwards, "Lawn Decoration," *Annual Report* 31 (1901), 248.

31. Huntley, "The Farmer's Dooryard," 62.

32. A. L. Hatch, "Discussion," *Annual Report* 25 (1895), 91.

33. Cleveland, *Landscape Architecture*, 44.

34. F. E. Pease, "Home, Planning and Planting the Grounds," *Annual Report* 32 (1902), 190.

35. Zona Gale, *Birth* (New York: The MacMillan Co., 1918), 224.

36. Mrs. William Habermann, "Why Not Build a Lattice?" *Wisconsin Horticulture* 6, no. 1 (September 1915), 203.

37. Carey, "Flighty Vistas," 37.

38. Cranefield, "The Improvement of Home Grounds," 267.

39. Mrs. Laura Smith, "Floriculture," *Transactions of the Wisconsin State Agricultural Society* 3 (1853), 257.

40. Mrs. I. H. Williams, "What Flowers Shall We Plant?" *Transactions* (1875), 174.

41. Frederic Cranefield, "Adornment of Home Grounds," *Annual Report* 25 (1895), 89.

42. Manning, *A Handbook for Planning and Planting Small Home Grounds*, 7.

43. O. S. Willey, "Ornamental Trees and Shrubs," *Transactions* (1870), 54.

44. Few cities and towns in Wisconsin had developed civic forestry programs before the 1920s; therefore, street planting and maintenance were the responsibility of the homeowner.

45. Ida E. Tilson, "Home Adornment," *Transactions* 16 (1886), 210, 211.

46. Adams, *Restoring American Gardens: An Encyclopedia of Heirloom Ornamental Plants, 1640–1940*, 104.

47. Ibid., 106.

48. Bailey, *Manual of Gardening*, 54–55. This statement accompanied the drawing on page 15.

49. Ramsdell, "Planning and Planting," 219.

50. William G. McLean, "Improve the Small Lot," *Annual Report* 42, part 1 (1912), 185.

51. Allen, "Garden Floriculture," 338, 341. Allen's suggestions for the type of plants to be used in this garden are included in chapter 5.

52. Mrs. D. Huntley, "The Flower Garden—Sowing and Transplanting," *Transactions* 10 (1880), 331–332.

53. James William Miller, "German Heirloom Gardening Research Report," 2002. Unpublished document, on file in the archives at Old World Wisconsin, Eagle, Wisconsin, 124.

54. Ibid., 125.

55. "Kitchen Garden," *Transactions* 1 (1851), 294.

56. "Annual Meeting: Annual Address," *Report of the Wisconsin State Horticultural Society for the Year 1869* (1870), 12.

57. J. S. Stickney, "How Best to Utilize Our Fruit," *Transactions* 8 (1878), 34.

58. Mrs. J. Montgomery Smith, "The Kitchen Garden," *Annual Report* 22 (1892), 157.

59. Ibid., 157.

60. "An Ideal Village Garden," *The Wisconsin Horticulturist* 2, no. 7 (September 1897), 8.

61. "A City Garden—One Man's Experience," *The Wisconsin Horticulturist* 5, no. 7 (September 1900), 12.

62. Irving Smith, "Discussion," *Annual Report* 41, part 1 (1911), 9.

63. McLean, "Improve the Small Lot," 186.

64. Cranefield, "The Improvement of Home Grounds," 296.

65. Mrs. D. C. Ayers, "Inexpensive Methods of Making Home Pleasant," *Transactions* 7 (1877), 51.

66. Membership lists sometimes included nurserymen's business cards. In 1904, thirty business members were listed.

67. Beal, "Ornamental Planting," 162.

68. Tilson, "Home Adornment," 212.

69. Manning, *A Handbook for Planning and Planting Small Home Grounds*. The plant catalog is a thirty-four-page addendum to the main body of text.

70. Ramsdell, "Planning and Planting," 215.

71. Ibid., 220.

72. The organization was formed in 1913. Jens Jensen and O. C. Simonds were two of the founding members.

Chapter 5

1. Mrs. D. C. Ayers, "Flowers for All," *Transactions of the Wisconsin State Horticultural Society* 9 (1879), 258.

2. Crawford, "Domestic Gardens in Southern Wisconsin," 81–107.

3. The years in which changes were made were 1893, 1894, 1904, 1905, 1915, 1920, and 1925.

4. "Recommended Varieties for Wisconsin," *Combined Annual Reports of the Wisconsin State Horticultural Society for the Years Ending July 1, 1927 and July 1, 1928* 57, 16.

5. Carolyn A. Strong, William A. Toole, and V. E. Brubaker, "Planning the Flower Garden: Varieties Recommended for Wisconsin by Special Committee," *Wisconsin Horticulture* 20, no. 8 (April 1930), 229.

6. George J. Kellogg, "Evergreens—Beauty and Utility," *Transactions* (1872), 171.

7. A. A. Arnold, "Evergreens," *Transactions* 10 (1880), 87.

8. W. D. Boynton, "Evergreens for Ornamental Purposes," *Annual Report* 28 (1898), 214.

9. Ibid., 215.

10. In Green Bay, it was not until 1920 that a city arborist was hired to take responsibility for street plantings; some smaller communities to this day do not have a comprehensive street planting program.

11. James Currie, "Some Hardy Shrubs," *Annual Report* 23 (1893), 103–110.

12. Ibid., 109.

13. "Black List," *Annual Report* 39 (1909), xliii.

14. Ibid., xliii–xliv.

15. The five articles that are combined in this pamphlet were presented by William Toole at WSHS annual meetings between 1919 and 1922. They are entitled "Domesticating Our Native Wild Flowers," "Our Native Shrubs of Wisconsin," "Our Wisconsin Native Trees," "Cultivation of Our Native Ferns," and "Our Native Climbing Vines."

16. *Nemophilia*, also known as baby blue eyes, is native to the western United States but not well known in Wisconsin gardens today.

17. Mrs. I. H. Williams, "What Flowers Shall We Plant?" *Transactions* (1875), 174–175.

18. Ayers, "Inexpensive Methods of Making Home Pleasant," 51.

19. Allen, "Garden Floriculture," 339–340.

20. Mrs. Irene H. Williams, "Garden Vases and Hanging Baskets," *Transactions* 7 (1877), 87.

21. For a complete list of annuals available in Wisconsin during the nineteenth century, refer to Crawford, "Domestic Gardens in Southern Wisconsin," appendix III, "Plants Used in Wisconsin During the Nineteenth Century," 196–210.

22. W. J. Moyle, "A Perennial Border," *Wisconsin Horticulture* 5, no. 2 (October 1914), 22.

23. The bulb catalog from the Ann Arbor, Michigan–based Old House Gardens is an excellent source for heirloom bulbs and their history.

24. Samuel Baxter, "Roses in Wisconsin," *Transactions* 14 (1884), 67.

25. Heirloom Roses Inc. (http://www.heirloomroses.com) and The Antique Rose Emporium (http://www.antiqueroseemporium.com) are two such nurseries.

26. Mrs. J. Montgomery Smith, "The Kitchen Garden," *Annual Report* 22 (1892), 155–159.

27. "Discussion," *Annual Report* 22 (1892), 159.

28. "Plant a Victory Garden," supplement, *Wisconsin Horticulture* 9, no 6. (February 1919), 3, 7, 11.

Chapter 6

1. Helen H. Charlton, "In the Garden," *Annual Report of the Wisconsin State Horticultural Society* 22 (1892), 161.

2. To access the Wisconsin Historical Society Library-Archives, visit http://www.wisconsinhistory.org/libraryarchives/.

3. Adams, *Restoring American Gardens*, 19.

4. "The Wauwatosa Historical Society's Kneeland-Walker House and Gardens," a handout from the Wauwatosa Historical Society.

5. Charles A. Birnbaum, "Preservation Brief 36: Protecting Cultural Landscapes: Planning, Treatment, and Management of Historic Landscapes" (Washington, DC: National Park Service, 1994); http://www.nps.gov/history/hps/tps/briefs/brief36.htm.

6. Mrs. H. M. Lewis, "The Adornment of Home," *Transactions of the Wisconsin State Horticultural Society* (1874), 47.

Selected Bibliography

Secondary Sources

America's Heartland: A Guide to Our Past. Eagle: Old World Wisconsin, 2003.

Adams, Denise W. *Restoring American Gardens: An Encyclopedia of Heirloom Ornamental Plants, 1640–1940*. Portland, OR: Timber Press, 2004.

Alanen, Arnold R., and Robert Melnick, eds. *Preserving Cultural Landscapes in America*. Baltimore: Johns Hopkins University Press, 2000.

Beveridge, Charles E. "Frederick Law Olmsted." In *American Landscape Architecture: Designers and Places*, edited by William E. Tishler. Washington, DC: The Preservation Press, 1989.

Birnbaum, Charles A., ed. *Guidelines for the Treatment of Cultural Landscapes*. Washington, DC: National Park Service, 2000.

———. "Preservation Brief 36: Protecting Cultural Landscapes: Planning, Treatment, and Management of Historic Landscapes." Washington, DC: National Park Service, 1994.

———, and Lisa Crowder, eds. *Pioneers of American Landscape Design*. Washington, DC: National Park Service, 1993.

Cain, Cortney A. "The Development of Horticulture in Wisconsin, 1850s–1950s: Case Studies of Bayfield, Crawford, and Door Counties." Master's thesis, Department of Landscape Architecture, University of Wisconsin–Madison, 2006.

Carmichael, Marcia C. *Putting Down Roots: Gardening Insights from Wisconsin's Early Settlers*. Madison: Wisconsin Historical Society Press, 2011.

Carstensen, Vernon. "The Origin and Early Development of the Wisconsin Idea." *Wisconsin Magazine of History* 39 (Spring 1956): 181–188. http://content.wisconsinhistory.org/u?/wmh,20550.

Carter, Thomas, and Elizabeth Collins Cromley. *Invitation to Vernacular Architecture: A Guide to the Study of Ordinary Buildings and Landscapes*. Knoxville: University of Tennessee Press, 2005.

Clark, Clifford Edward. *The American Family Home, 1800–1960*. Chapel Hill: University of North Carolina Press, 1986.

Crawford, Sharon D. "The Development and Evolution of Domestic Gardens in Southern Wisconsin during the Nineteenth Century." Master's thesis, Department of Landscape Architecture, University of Wisconsin–Madison, 1983.

———. "Pioneer Wisconsin Gardens." *Wisconsin Academy Review* 30 (September 1984): 3–8.

Creswell, John W. *Research Design: Qualitative & Quantitative Approaches*. Thousand Oaks, CA: Sage Publications, 1994.

Duchscherer, Paul, and Douglas Keister. *Outside the Bungalow: America's Arts and Crafts Garden*. New York: Penguin Studio, 1999.

Favretti, Rudy L. *For Every House a Garden*. Hanover: University Press of New Hampshire, 1990.

Foy, Jessica H., and Thomas J. Schlereth, eds. *American Home Life, 1880–1930: A Social History of Space and Services*. Knoxville: University of Tennessee Press, 1992.

Grese, Robert. "Bailey, Liberty Hyde." In *Pioneers of American Landscape Design: An Annotated Bibliography*, edited by Charles Birnbaum and Lisa Crowder. Washington, DC: U.S. Department of the Interior, National Park Service, 1993.

Haeger, John. *Men and Money: The Urban Frontier at Green Bay, 1815–1840*. Mount Pleasant: Clarke Historical Library, Central Michigan University, 1970.

Hayden, Dolores. *Redesigning the American Dream: The Future of Housing, Work, and Family Life*. New York: W. W. Norton, 2002.

Heritage Hill State Historical Park. "Fort Howard Interpretive Plan," 2000. On file in the archives of Heritage Hill State Historical Park, Green Bay, WI.

Hill, May Brawley. *Grandmother's Garden: The Old-Fashioned American Garden*. New York: Harry N. Abrams Inc., 1995.

Hunt, John Dixon, and Joachim Wolschke-Bulmann, eds. *The Vernacular Garden*. Washington, DC: Dumbarton Oaks, 1993.

Jackson, John Brinckerhoff. *A Sense of Place, A Sense of Time*. New Haven, CT: Yale University Press, 1994.

———. *Discovering the Vernacular Landscape*. New Haven, CT: Yale University Press, 1984.

———. *The Necessity for Ruins and Other Topics*. Amherst: University of Massachusetts Press, 1980.

———. "Past and Present." In *The Vernacular Garden*, edited by John Dixon Hunt and Joachim Wolschke-Bulmann. Washington, DC: Dumbarton Oaks, 1993.

Leighton, Ann. *American Gardens of the Nineteenth Century: For Comfort and Affluence*. Amherst: University of Massachusetts Press, 1987.

———. *American Gardens in the Eighteenth Century: For Use or for Delight*. Boston: Houghton Mifflin, 1976.

Lynch, Kevin. *What Time Is This Place?* Cambridge, MA: MIT Press, 1972.

McBride, Genevieve G. *Women's Wisconsin: From Native Matriarchies to the New Millennium*. Madison: Wisconsin Historical Society Press, 2005.

Miller, James William. "German Heirloom Gardening Research Report." 2002. Transcript on file in the Archives Department, Old World Wisconsin, Eagle, WI.

Milspaw, Yvonne. "Landscape Patterns in a Small Town: Visible Normality Within the Epic Laws of the Folk Landscape." Paper presented to the American Folklore Society, Albuquerque, NM, October 10, 1993.

Murtagh, William J. *Keeping Time: The History and Theory of Preservation in America*. New York: John Wiley, 2006.

Ostergren, Robert C., and Thomas R. Vale, eds. *Wisconsin Land and Life*. Madison: University of Wisconsin Press, 1997.

Peterson, Fred W. *Homes in the Heartland: Balloon Frame Farmhouses of the Upper Midwest, 1850–1920*. Lawrence: University Press of Kansas, 1992.

Punch, Walter, ed. *Keeping Eden: A History of Gardening in America*. Boston: Little, Brown and Company, 1992.

Rahmlow, Henry J., and the Wisconsin Apple and Horticultural Society. *One Hundred Years: The Wisconsin State Horticultural Society, 1868–1968*. Madison: Wisconsin Apple and Horticultural Council, 1968.

————, and the Wisconsin State Horticultural Society. *A History of Seventy-Five Years of Service by the Wisconsin State Horticultural Society*. Madison: Wisconsin State Horticultural Society, 1943.

Schroeder, Fred E. H. *Front Yard America: The Evolution and Meaning of a Vernacular Domestic Landscape*. Bowling Green, OH: Bowling Green State University Popular Press, 1993.

Scott-James, Anne. *The Cottage Garden*. Middlesex, England: Allen Lane, 1981.

Smith, Mary L. P. *Eben E. Rexford: A Biographical Sketch; a Memorial Containing "Silver Threads Among the Gold" and His Last Poem*. Philadelphia: J. B. Lippincott Company, 1917.

Speltz, Mark. "An Interest in Health and Happiness as Yet Untold: The Woman's Club of Madison, 1893–1917." *Wisconsin Magazine of History* 89, no. 3 (Spring 2006): 2–15.

Steele, Fletcher. *Gardens and People*. Boston: Houghton Mifflin, 1964.

Tice, Patricia M. *Gardening in America, 1830–1910*. Rochester, NY: Strong Museum, 1984.

————. "Gardens of Change." In *American Home Life, 1880–1930: A Social History of Space and Services*, edited by Jessica H. Foy and Thomas J. Schlereth, 190–208. Knoxville: University of Tennessee Press, 1992.

Tishler, William H., ed. *Midwestern Landscape Architecture*. Urbana: University of Illinois Press, in cooperation with the Library of American Landscape History, 2000.

————. *American Landscape Architecture: Designers and Places*. Washington, DC: The Preservation Press, 1989.

Watts, May Theilgaard. *Reading the Landscape of America*. New York: Macmillan, 1975.

Weishan, Michael. *The New Traditional Garden: A Practical Guide to Creating and Restoring Authentic American Gardens for Homes of All Ages*. New York: Ballantine Publishing Group, 1999.

Wilson, William H. *The City Beautiful Movement: Creating the North American Landscape*. Baltimore: Johns Hopkins University Press, 1989.

Wisconsin Cartographers' Guild, ed. *Wisconsin's Past and Present: A Historical Atlas*. Madison: University of Wisconsin Press, 2002.

Wright, Gwendolyn. *Building the Dream: A Social History of Housing in America*. New York: Pantheon Books, 1981.

Zaniewski, Kazmierz, and Carol Rosen. *Atlas of Ethnic Diversity in Wisconsin*. Madison: University of Wisconsin Press, 1988.

Primary Sources

Bailey, Liberty Hyde. *Manual of Gardening; A Practical Guide to the Making of Home Grounds and the Growing of Flowers, Fruits, and Vegetables for Home Use*. New York: Macmillan Co., 1910.

———. *Garden-making: Suggestions for the Utilizing of Home Grounds*. Garden-Craft Series. New York, London: Macmillan, 1898.

Breck, Joseph. *The Flower-Garden, or Breck's Book of Flowers; in which are Described All the Herbaceous Perennials, Annuals, Shrubby Plants and Evergreen Trees Desirable for Ornamental Purposes, with Directions for Their Cultivation*. Boston: John P. Jewitt & Co., 1851.

Cleveland, H. W. S. *Landscape Architecture, As Applied to the Wants of the West*. Chicago: Jansen, McClurg & Co., 1873. Reprint edited by Roy Lubove. Pittsburgh: University of Pittsburgh Press, 1965.

Downing, A. J. *A Treatise on the Theory and Practice of Landscape Gardening, Adapted to North America; with a View to the Improvement of Country Residences*, 6th ed. New York: A. O. Moore, 1859.

———. *Cottage Residences; or, A Series of Designs for Rural Cottages and Cottage Villas, and Their Gardens and Grounds. Adapted to North America*, 3rd ed. New York: Wiley and Putnam, 1847.

Earle, Alice Morse. *Old Time Gardens*. New York: The Macmillan Company, 1901.

Elliott, F. R. *Hand Book of Practical Landscape Gardening: Designed for City and Suburban Residence, and Country School-Houses, Containing Designs for Lots and Grounds from a Lot 30 x 100 Feet to a 40 Acre Plot*. Rochester, NY: D. M. Dewey, 1881.

"Frederic Cranefield, Long Ill, Dies at 73," *Capital Times*, 1939. MSS 1003, box 1-5 MAD 3/57/F4, folder MAD 3/71/G3, Wisconsin Historical Society Library-Archives, Madison.

Gale, Zona. *Birth*. New York: The McMillan Company, 1918.

———. "Civic Improvement in the Little Towns." Washington, DC: American Civic Association, 1913.

Hutchinson, Frances Kinsley. *Our Country Home: How We Transformed a Wisconsin Woodland*. Chicago: A.C. McClurg & Co., 1908.

Jekyll, Gertrude. *Color Schemes for the Flower Garden*. London: Country Life Ltd., 1908. Reprint, New Hampshire: Ayers Company, 1983.

Kellaway, Herbert J. *How to Lay Out Suburban Home Grounds*. New York: John Wiley & Sons Inc., 1915.

King, Louise Yeoman. "Editor's Preface." In *Design in the Little Garden*, by Fletcher Steele. Boston: The Atlantic Monthly Press, 1924.

Manning, Warren H. *A Handbook for Planning and Planting Small Home Grounds*. Menomonie, WI: Stout Manual Training School, 1899.

Miller, Wilhelm. *The Prairie Spirit in Landscape Gardening*. Circular 184. Urbana: University of Illinois Agricultural Experiment Station, 1915.

Oakey, Alexander F. *Home Grounds*. New York: D. Appleton's Home Books, Appleton and Company, 1881.

Parsons, Samuel, Jr. *How to Plan the Home Grounds*. New York: Doubleday & McClure Co., 1899.

"Pro' Fruit Men Oust Cranefield Because He Wanted to Help Amateurs." *Capital Times*, November 15, 1926. MSS 1003, box 1-5 MAD 3/57/F4, folder MAD 3/71/G3. Wisconsin Historical Society Library-Archives, Madison.

Rexford, Eben E. *A-B-C of Gardening*. Harper's A-B-C Series. New York, London: Harper & Brothers, 1915.

———. *A-B-C of Vegetable Gardening*. Harper's A-B-C Series. New York: Harper & Brothers, 1916.

———. *Amateur Gardencraft: A Book for the Home-Maker and Garden Lover*. Philadelphia: J. B. Lippincott Company, 1912.

———. *Flowers, How to Grow Them*. Philadelphia: Penn Publishing Company, 1898.

———. *Four Seasons in the Garden*. Philadelphia & London: J. B. Lippincott Company, 1907.

———. *Home Floriculture: A Familiar Guide to the Treatment of Flowering and Other Ornamental Plants in the House and Garden*. Rochester, NY: J. Vick, 1890.

———. *The Home Garden: A Book on Vegetable and Small-Fruit Growing, for the Use of the Amateur Gardener*. Philadelphia: J. B. Lippincott Company, 1918.

———. *Indoor Gardening*. Philadelphia: J. B. Lippincott Company, 1910.

———. *The Making of a Home*. Philadelphia: G. W. Jacobs & Company, 1916.

Schafer, Joseph. *A History of Agriculture in Wisconsin*. Madison: State Historical Society of Wisconsin, 1922. http://digital.library.wisc.edu/1711.dl/WI.HistAgSchaf.

Scott, Frank J. *The Art of Beautifying Suburban Home Grounds of Small Extent: The Advantage of Suburban Homes over City or Country Homes; The Comfort and Economy of Neighboring Improvements; The Choice and Treatment of Building Sites; and the Best Modes of Laying Out, Planting and Keeping Decorated Grounds*. New York: D. Appleton & Co., 1870.

Simonds, O. C. *Landscape-Gardening*. Rural Science Series. New York: The Macmillan Company, 1920.

Snyder, Van Vechten & Co. *Historical Atlas of Wisconsin: Embracing Complete State and County Maps, City & Village Plats, Together with Separate State and County Histories: Also Special Articles on the Geology, Education, Agriculture, and Other Important Interests of the State*. Milwaukee: Snyder, Van Vechten & Co., 1878.

Steele, Fletcher. *Design in the Little Garden*. Boston: The Atlantic Monthly Press, 1924.

Stickley, Gustav. *Craftsman Homes*. New York: Craftsman Publishing Company, 1909.

Tabor, Grace. *The Landscape Gardening Book*. Philadelphia: The John C. Winston Company, 1911.

Toole, William. *Native Plants of Wisconsin Suitable for Cultivation*. Madison: Wisconsin State Horticultural Society, 1922.

Weidenmann, Jacob. *Beautifying Country Homes*. New York: Orange Judd and Company, 1870.

Wisconsin State Horticultural Society. *Wisconsin Horticulture*. Madison: Wisconsin State Horticultural Society, 1910–1967.

———. *Transactions of the Wisconsin State Horticultural Society*. Madison: Wisconsin State Horticultural Society, 1869–1889. http://digital.library.wisc.edu/1711.dl/WI.USAIN.

———. *Annual Report of the Wisconsin State Horticultural Society*. Madison: Wisconsin State Horticultural Society, 1890–1928. http://digital.library.wisc.edu/1711.dl/WI.USAIN.

Wisconsin State Horticultural Society, and University of Wisconsin–Madison Libraries. *The Wisconsin Horticulturist*. Madison: Wisconsin State Horticultural Society, 1896–1903. http://digital.library.wisc.edu/1711.dl/WI.USAIN.

Index

Page locators in *italics* indicate photographs and drawings.

Abbott, Charles S., 46
Achillea the Pearl, 116
Achyranthus, 112
Adams, Denise Wiles, 84, 119, 127
Allen, Dr. H., 59, 86–87, 112–113
alpine gardens, 94–95, *95*
alternanthera, 115
amaranth, 110
Amaranthus caudatus, 6
American arborvitae, 104
'American Beauty' rose, 119
American Civic Association, 20
American elm, 106, *107*
American ivy, 120
American Rose Society, 119
American Society of Landscape Architects, 9, 11
Ampelopsis quinquefolia, 120
Ampelopsis tricuspidata, 120
Ampelopsis vine, *16, 17, 90,* 120
Annual Report of the Wisconsin State Horticultural Society, xvii, 43–45, 60, 61, 102, 141
annuals: at Cotton House at Heritage Hill State Historical Park, 6; in cutout beds, 7, 80, 81, 98, 124; flower bed placement and, 86; at Mitchell estate, 52, 55; preferred uses for, 88, *112*; recommended, 102, 109–119; Rexford and, 15, *121*
'Apothecary Rose' (*Rosa gallica officinalis*), *120*
aquilegia, 116
arborvitae, 104, 105
Arends, George, 123

Arnold, A. A., 46, 104
The Art of Beautifying Suburban Home Grounds of Small Extent (Scott), 7
artemesia, 115
artillery plant, 115
asparagus, 90
asters, *xiv,* 23, 88, 112, 113, 116
Astilbe 'Fanal,' *136*
Aust, Franz, 11, 96
'Autumn Joy' sedum, *123*
Ayers, Mrs. D. C., 96, 101, 112
azaleas, 109

bachelor buttons, 116
back garden, *87, 91*
Bailey, Liberty Hyde, xix, 13–15, 17, 61, 84, 94
balsam, *xiv,* 88, 104, 110, 113
Barber, Samuel, *32*
barberry, 76, *107*
barley, *27*
Bass, William, 132
basswood trees, 105
Beal, Professor, 98
beans, 1, 90, 122
Beaumont, William, 25
beautification of home grounds: boundary and fencing elements and, 74–79; differentiation of space and, 61–74; flower bed placement and, 86–88; introduction to, 59–61; lawn, path, and driveway appearance and, 79–81; native plant use and, 95–100; shrub placement and, 84–86; specialty gardens and, 94–95; tree placement and, 81–83; vegetable garden placement and, 90–93; vine use and, 88–90

Beautifying Country Homes (Weidenmann), 5, 7

beets, 28, 90, 122

begonia, 115

Belgian Farm at Heritage Hill State Historical Park, *133*

bell worts, 98

birch trees, 105, 106

Birnbaum, Charles, 132–133

bitter sweet, 76, 112

"black list" plants, 109

black spruce, 104

bleeding heart, 109, 116

blood-roots, 98

Bloomsdale Savoy spinach, 122

blue mistflower, *123*

Blue Spruce, 105

blue violets, 98

Boerner, Alfred L., 74

boltonia latisquama, 116

Boston ivy, 120

boundary elements, 74–79

box elder, 105

Boynton, W. D., 105

brasella rubra, 115

Breck, Joseph, 11

broccoli, 122

brochures, 128, *128*

browallia, 110

buckeye, 106

burdock, 15, *15*, 30

Burten, Carla, home of, *34*

butterfly flower, 23

cabbage, 90, 91, 122

caladium, *6*, 22, 110

Campbell, Mrs. Vie H., 48, 76

candy-tuft, 110, 112

canna lilies, *6*, 7, 22, 113, *130*

Carey, C. E., 72

carpet beds: Allen and, 86; Breck and, 11; in Cranefield design, 68; in garden evolution, 18,
59, 88, 124; at Mitchell estate, 55; nurseries and, 98; overview of, 7; patterns of, *6*; Rexford and, 15; Steele and Tabor on, 22; use of, 8; as "Victorian" element, *38*

carrots, 28, 122

castor bean plants, 7, 15, *112*

Catalpa spicrosa, 105

'Catherine Becker' dahlia, *114*

cauliflower, 122

cedar, 104, 105

celery, 122

celosia, *6*

centaurea, 115

Chantenay carrot, 122

Charlton, Helen H., 125

city planning, 7–9, 26, 67

civic enhancement organizations, 20, 42

civic improvement movement, 49–51

clematis, 120, *121*, *137*, 138

Clematis tangutica, *137*

Cleveland, Horace William Shaler, 7–9, 63, 77

cocolobia, 115

Coe, Converse & Edwards Co. nursery, 103

coleus, *6*, 15, *15*, 22, 110, 112, *112*, 115

Coleus Verschaffeltii, 112

Colonial nostalgia, 12–13

columbine, 116

community planning, 7–9, 26, 67

coneflower, *137*

Convolvulus minor, 87, 110

corn, 1, 25, 27, 28, 90, 91, 122

"cottage garden," 1, 2, 30, *134*

Cotton House at Heritage Hill State Historical Park, *6*

crab apple trees, 105

The Craftsman, 10, 20

Craftsman house, 20–21

Cranefield, Frederic: on boundaries of farm homes, 75–76; on children and gardens, 56; fruit industry and, 51; on garden layout and composition, 61, 63, 68–69; garden models of, 96, *96*; life and career of, 49–50; native plant use and, 124; on overplanting, 83; on planting shrubs, 84, 85–86; recommends Manning's *Handbook*, 9; on rock gardens, 94; suggestions for rural landscape, *69*; suggestions for village lot, *70*; on tree placement, 83; as WSHS executive secretary, 9, 49, 51, 61, 109; on yard design, 79, *79*, 80, 81

Crawford, Sharon D., 28–39, 41, 96, 102

'Cri de Coeur' tulip, *117*

'Crimson Rambler' rose, *120*

Crosby's Egyptian beet, 122

Crossroads at Big Creek, 138, *139*

Currie, James, 107

cutout beds, 5, 15, 37, 39, 81

Dahl, Andreas Larsen, xix, 25, 32–35, 37, 38, 65, 66, 82, 132

dahlias, 113, *114*, 115

dairy farming, 37–39

daisies, 34, *38*, 116

dandelions, 15

daphne, 109

date, interpretive, 129

datura, 113

daylilies, 13, 109

deciduous trees, 105–106, 122

delphiniums, *89*, 116

Department of Horticulture (University of Wisconsin), 11, 13, 49, 63

'Deuil de Paul Fontaine' rose, 119

dianthus, *xvii*, 116

Dicentra Spectabilis, 116

dicentras, 98, 116

differentiation of space, 61–74

Dirst, Victoria, 114

dogwood, 107, 109

'Dorothy Perkins' rose, *120*

double portulaca, 113

Downing, Andrew Jackson, 1, 3, 51, 61, 62, 84

driveways: borders for, *89*, 124; Cranefield and, 68, 69, 81; Edwards on, 67; in garden evolution, 19, 22, 96, 97; at Mitchell estate, 55; Niles and, 72; Pease on, 77; in professional landscaping plan,

74; shrub placement and, 84; "Victorian" elements and, 38; in Weidenmann plan, 5; WSHS recommendations on, 61

dwarf juniper, 105

Earle, Alice Morse, 13, 14, 17, 88

Edwards, F. C., 67, 76

eggplant, 122

Eliot, Charles, 84

Elizabethan gardens, 94

elm trees, 105, 106

Engelman ivy, 120

English Gothic Style cottage design, *3*

English-style elements, 74

ethnic farm gardens, *134*

Euonymus, 107

euphorbia, 113

evergreen trees, 104–105, 122

farmsteads, *24*, 28–30, *29*, 55, 56

fencing elements, 74–79

ferns, 98, 112, 115

feverfew, 6

Firth, Sue, 2

flower beds, 37, 79–81, 86–88

The Flower-Garden (Breck), 11

forget-me-not, 23

fort gardens, 25

foundation planting: Bailey and, 15; Cranefield and, 68, 69, 85; evergreens in, 105; example of, *95*; function of, 22, 58; in garden evolution, 19, 21, *21*, 96; at Hooker home, *34*; at Hutchinson family home, *57*; Manning and, 9, 64; Niles and, 72; Scott and Weidenmann and, 74; at Secor home, *110*; shrubs in, 84–86, 109, 123, 129

fruit industry, 43, 46, 51

fruit trees: availability of, 30; on "Black List," 109; in Cranefield design, 70–72; in garden evolution, 18; Olmstead on, 27, 28; placement of, 90–92; recommendations for, 61, 63, 102; in typical gardens, 1

fuchsia, 115

Gale, Zona, 20, 77
gardening: increased popularity of, 102; planning and, 128–135; researching, 125–127; satisfaction in, 125
gardening journals and magazines, 10
'Gem of the Prairies' rose, 119
gentian, 23
geography, evolution of Wisconsin, 23–28
George Arends Nursery, 123
geraniums, 53, 80, 110, 113, 115
German immigrants, 27, 39–41, 90
German iris, 116
German peasant gardens, 39–41
glaciation, 23–25
gladiolus, 113, 115
globe arborvitae, 105
gnaphalium, 115
Goff, Emmet S., 49, 50, 63
golden arborvitae, 105
golden rods, 23
Gothic Revival cottage, 54, 55
Gothic style, 62
grandmother's gardens, 12–13, 14, 88
grape ivy, 28, 120
grape vines, 91, 112
green ash trees, 105

Haasch, E. E., home of, 126
Hamilton, William, 2
A Handbook for Planning and Planting Small Home Grounds (Manning), 9, 63–64, 85, 109
Harris, J. S., 122
Hatch, A. L., 76–77
Hauge, Halvor Nerison, home of, 36
hawthorn, 75, 106
hedges, 56, 64, 74–78, 104, 105, 107
hemp, 27
'Henri Martin' rose, 119
hepaticas, 98
herb gardens, 94
Heritage Flower Farm, 14, 123, 136, 137

Heritage Hill State Historical Park, xiii, 6, 120, 133, 133, 134
Hislop, Thomas, 62, 74–75, 76
Hobbins, Joseph, 51–53, 91
hollyhocks, 13, 18, 116
home grounds, beautification of: boundary and fencing elements and, 74–79; differentiation of space and, 61–74; flower bed placement and, 86–88; introduction to, 59–61; lawn, path, and driveway appearance and, 79–81; native plant use and, 95–100; shrub placement and, 84–86; specialty gardens and, 94–95; tree placement and, 81–83; vegetable garden placement and, 90–93; vine use and, 88–90
home placement, 61–74
honeysuckle, 13, 53, 76, 107, 120, 121, 138
Hooker, Henry, home of, 35
The Horticulturist, 3
houseleeks, 22
Hovey's golden arborvitae, 105
Huntley, Mrs. D., 43, 46, 76, 87–88
Hutchinson, Frances Kinsley, 58
Hutchinson family, 57
hydrangea, 107

ice plant, 22
immigration, 27, 29, 39–42, 90
individuality, in the garden, 56–58
information, distribution of, 132–135
interaction, between people and gardens, 56–58
interpretive date, 129
interpretive plan, 130–131, 132–133
iris, 18, 31, 109, 116
ivy, 53, 76, 115, 120

James Vick Seed Company, 119
Jefferson, Thomas, 2
Jekyll, Gertrude, 13, 17, 21, 74, 88
Jensen, Jens, xix, 9–10, 96, 99
joe-pye weed, 137
John A. Salzer Seed Company, 102, 120, 140
Johnny-jump-ups, 18

Johnson, Mary C. C., 48

journals, 10

juneberry, 106

juniper, 104, 105

Kellogg, George J., 104

Kelton House Farm, *89*

Kenilworth Ivy, 115

Kentucky coffee tree, 105

Kerr, Mrs. Prof. A., 48

Kneeland-Walker House, *60*, 131, *137*

kudzu, *121*

Lady Washington, 113

landscape, evolution of Wisconsin, 23–28, 37–39

landscape architecture: defined, 7; development of discipline, 11, 72–74; landscape gardening and, 13

Landscape Architecture, As Applied to the Wants of the West (Cleveland), 7, 9, 63

landscape plan(s): Cranefield and, 61, 70, *70*; developing, 128, 130–133, 135; Manning and, 98; Niles and, *71*; Scott and Weidenmann and, 74; sharing, 127; for Villa Louis, 129; Weidenmann and, 5

lantanas, 113

larkspur, 109

lattice fence, 78, *78*

lawns: boundaries and, 74, 75, 76, 77; Cranefield and, 68, 82; Edwards on, 67; in garden evolution, 12, 19, 30, 37; in garden models, 96; manicured, *118*, *126*; Manning and, 63–64; at Mitchell estate, 53, 55; Scott and, 7; shrub placement and, 84, *107*; Simonds and, 50; space differentiation and, 62; Steele and, 22; tree placement and, 105; "Victorian" elements and, 39; in Weidenmann plan, *4*, 5, *5*; WSHS recommendations on, 79–81

lemon lilies, 116

lettuce, 122

Lewis, Charlotte, 48, 138

Lewis and Clark expedition, 2, 25

liatris, *137*

lilacs, 13, 18, 29, 34, 76, 107, 124

lilies, *31*, *89*, 109, 116

lily of the valley, 109

linden trees, 105, 106

lobelia, 115

Longnecker, William, 11

lupines, *118*

Madeira vine, 87, 115

Madison Park and Pleasure Association, 42

magazines, 10

'Magna Charta' rose, 119

The Making of a Home (Rexford), 17

Malisch, Mrs. R. H., 94

Manning, Warren H.: career of, 9; Cranefield and, 61; on differentiation of space, 63–64; native plant use and, 95, 98, 109, 124; Ramsdell and, 62, 81, 85, 99; Steele and, 21; on yard design, 81

maple trees, 105, 106

marigolds, 6, 135

Marshall, Samuel, 49

maurandya, 115

McGuire, Diane Kostial, 2

McLean, William G., 86, 92

Meissner, Adolf, 41

mignonette, *xvii*, 110, 112

military fort gardens, 25

Miller, James William, 39, 41, 90

Miller, Wilhelm, xix, 99, 100

miniature gardens, 94

Mitchell, Alexander, estate of, 39, *52*, 53–55, 58

Mitchell, Mrs. Alexander, 55

M'Mahon, Bernard, 2

moccasin flower, 23

mock oyster, 93

moneywort, 115

Moore, James G., 85

morning glory, 87, 110, 120, *121*, 138

'Mrs. John Laing' rose, 119

nasturtiums, *102*, 110, 120, *121*, *170*

native plants, 95–100, 109, *116*, 124

nemophilia, 110

Niles, E. H., 69–72, *70*, *71*

Norway maple, 106, *106*

Norway spruce, 104

nostalgic gardens, 12–13, *14*, 88

nurseries, 29, 30, 55, 95, 98, 102, *103*, 109, 119

oak trees, 105, 106

objectives, for your vintage garden, 131

okra, 122

Old World Wisconsin, *29*, 39, *40*, 133, *134*, 135

Olmstead, Clarence W., 27–28, 37–39

Olmsted, Frederick Law, 3–5

onions, 28, 90, 122

orchard placement, 90–93

Oriental poppies, 116

Osage Orange, 75

Ostergren, Robert, 41

overplanting, 81–83

"Page Fence," 75, 76

painted cup, 23

pansies, *xviii*, 80, 88, 110, 112, 113, 115

parsnip, 122

Parthenocissus quinquefolia, 17, 120

Parthenocissus tricuspidata, 120

pathways: Allen and, 81, 86–87; in back garden, *87*; boardwalks, *107*; borders for, 41, 55; in Breck designs, 11; Cleveland on, 63; in Cranefield design, 68; Crawford and, 37; in Dahl photographs, 33, 34, *65*; in garden evolution, 22; in garden models, 96; at Heritage Hill State Historical Park's Tank Cottage garden, *134*; at Kneeland-Walker House, 131; in nostalgic gardens, 13; Pease on, 77; placement of, 67; plantings beside, 53, 88, 124; at Secor home, *110*; Smith on, 79; in "traditional" gardens, 30, *31*; on *Transactions* frontispiece, 56; "Victorian" elements and, 39; views on, 81; in Weidenmann plan, 5; WSHS recommendations on, 61; at Wychwood, 57

peas, 90, 122

peasant gardens, 39–41

Pease, F. E., 77, 85

pelargoniums, 113

peonies, 18, *31*, 34, 109, *111*, 135

perennials: in borders, 89; in "cottage gardens," 2; in Dahl photographs, *31*, 33, 65; in foundation planting, *86*; in garden evolution, 18, 22, 124; at Heritage Flower Farm, *137*; Hobbins on, 53; at Mitchell estate, 55; native, 29, 86, 95–96; in nostalgic gardens, 13; Rexford and, *16*, 17; rise in popularity of, 88; threats to, 129; in *Vick's Home Floriculture*, 15; WSHS recommendations on, 103, 109–119

'Perpetual White Moss' rose, 119

Petranek, E. A., 72

petunias, *xix*, 6, 112, 115

phlox, 13, 23, 88, 98, 109, 110, 112, 113, 115, 116

pin oak trees, 106

pine trees, 104, 105

pinks, 112, 116

pioneer gardens, 29

plans, for gardens, 128–135

plants, recommended: annual and perennial flowers, 109–119; deciduous trees, 105–106; evergreen trees, 101–104; introduction to, 101–104; roses, 119; shrubs, 107–109; vegetables, 122; vines, 120

platycodon, 116

Pollard, Joseph, 55

poplars, 105

poppy, 109, 116

potatoes, 27, 28, 90, 91

prairie garden, *116*

'Prairie Queen' rose, 119

"Prairie style" landscape, xix

"Preservation Brief 36" (Birnbaum), 132–133

primrose, 116

Primula Officinalis, 116

privet, 109

Progressive Era, 17–20, 92

pumpkins, 28

Pyrethrum aurea, *112*

pyrethrum roseum, 116

radishes, 122, *122*

rambler roses, *120*

Ramsdell, Charles, 62, 64, 81, 85, 98–99

ranunculus, 116

recommended plants: annual and perennial flowers, 109–119; deciduous trees, 105–106; evergreen trees, 104–105; introduction to, 101–104; roses, 119; shrubs, 107–109; vegetables, 122; vines, 120

reconstruction of gardens, 133

Red Cedar, 105

rehabilitation of gardens, 133

researching gardens, 125–127, 131

restoration of gardens, 133

Restoring American Gardens: An Encyclopedia of Heirloom Ornamental Plants, 1640–1940 (Adams), 119

Rexford, Eben: on *Ampelopsis* vine, *16*, 17, 90; on back garden, 87; on borders, 89; life and career of, 15–17; plant recommendations of, 108, 113, 121; publications of, xix; on rock gardens, 94; shrub placement and, 84, 86

ricinus, 110

Roby, H. W., 47

rock gardens, 94–95, *95*

Roloff, E. L., garden of, *117*

Rorer, Mrs., 93

roses: in garden evolution, 18, 19, 124; Hobbins on, 53; Huntley on, 76; Lewis on, 138; at Mitchell estate, 55; native, 98; in nostalgic gardens, 13; at Secor home, *110*; suggested, 103, 109, 119, *120*

running cypress, 87

Rural Gothic Style cottage design, *3*

'Russell's Cottage' rose, 119

Russian mulberry, 105

'Russian Virgin's Bower,' *137*

rustic fence, 76

rutabaga, 122

rye, 27

'Salet' rose, 119

salsify, 93

Salzer, John A. *See* John A. Salzer Seed Company

Schafer, Joseph, 41–42

Schlegelmilch House garden, site brochure for, *128*

Schottler Farm, *134*

Schulz, Charles and Auguste, home of, *40*

Scott, Frank J., xix, 7, 8, 51

Secor, Martin M., home of, *110*

sedum, *123*

'Seven Sisters' rose, 119

Shakespeare, William, 57

Shakespeare gardens, 94

shrubs, 84–86, 107–109, 122–124

Simonds, O. C., xix, 9–10, 49–50, 96, 99

Sisson's Peony Gardens, *111*

site brochures, 127, 128, *128*

smilax, 115

Smith, Irving, 92

Smith, Laura, 30, 79, 96

Smith, Mrs. J. Montgomery, 91, 122

smoke tree, 107

social reform movement, 42, 46

space differentiation, 61–74

specialty gardens, 94–95

spinach, 122

Spiraea x vanhouttei, 76, *108*

spirea Thunbergii, 76

spireas, 76, 108, 124

spring beauties, 98

spruce, 104, 105

squash, 1, 25

Steele, Fletcher, 21–22, 78

Stickley, Gustav, 20

strawberry tree, upright, 107

suburban homes and landscapes: boundary and fencing elements and, 76; Boynton and, 105; Cranefield and, 61, 68, *70*; Olmsted and Vaux and, 3; plans for, *4–5*, 8; Scott and, 7; Weidenmann and, 5; WSHS recommendations on, 56 sumac, 109

sweet alyssum, 110

sweet peas, *xx*, 110, 113, *121*

Tabor, Grace, 17, 21, 22, 78

Tank Cottage garden, *134*

Thornton, Tamara Plakins, 46

Tice, Patricia, 21

Tilson, Ida, 23, 83, 98

tomatoes, 122

Toole, William, *44*, 95, 99, 100, 109, 124, 127

topiary, 7, 8

"traditional" garden, 30, 31

Transactions of the Wisconsin State Horticultural Society: Allen excerpt in, 59; civic improvement and, 49, 60; frontispieces of, 53–56; Mitchell estate in, *52*; native plant use and, 98; overview of, xvii; publications of, 45; recommendations in, 102; WSHS activities and, 44

A Treatise on the Theory and Practice of Landscape Gardening Adapted to North America (Downing), 3

trees: placement of, 81–83; recommended, 104–106, 122. *See also* fruit trees

trends: changes in, 59–61; recommended by WSHS, 51–58

trilliums, 98

tritoma, 115

tropical beds, *6, 7*, 15, 110, *112*, *130*

tuberose, 113

tulips, 113, *117*

turnips, 28, 122

University of Wisconsin Department of Horticulture, 11, 13, 49, 63

upright strawberry tree, 107

urban garden model, 96–97, *97*

Utter, Delbert, 67

Van Schaick, Charles, xix, *132*

Vaux, Calvert, 3

vegetable gardens, 90–93, 102, 122, *133, 134*

verbena, 13, 53, 80, 110, 113, 115

vernacular garden: defined, xv, 19; evolution of, 39; "typical," 127

Vick, James, 15, 41, 119

'Vick's Caprice' rose, 119

Vick's Home Floriculture (Rexford), 15, 17

Vick's Monthly Magazine, 15, *122*

"Victorian" elements, in vernacular gardens, 38, 39

"Victorian" garden model, 96–97, *97*

victory gardens, 50–51, 92, 122

Villa Louis: landscape at, *6*, *130*; records of, 129, *129*

vinca, 115

vines: architecture and, *21*; Ayers on, 112; boundary and fencing elements and, 76, 79, 101; in "cottage gardens," 2; Cranefield and, 56; in Dahl photographs, 65, 66; in garden evolution, 124; at Hooker home, 34; Huntley on, x, 43; in immigrant gardens, 41; Manning on, 64; native, 50; Rexford and, 17, *121*; at Secor home, *110*; Tilson on, 98; in *Transactions* frontispiece, 55; in typical gardens, 1; use of, 88–90, 120; "Victorian" elements and, 39; at Wychwood, 58

vintage gardens, planning, 128–135

violets, 98, 116

Virginia creeper, 17, 53, 120

walkways. *See* pathways

war gardens, 50–51, 92, 102, 122

Washington, George, 2

Watts, May Theilgaard, 18–19, 97

Weidenmann, Jacob, 4, 5–7, 51, 61, 77

weigela, 107

wheat, 27, 37

white cedar, 104

Williams, Henry T., 47

willows, 105, 106

windbreaks, 104–105

Wisconsin Federation of Women's Clubs, 42

Wisconsin Garden Club Federation, 48, 51

Wisconsin Horticulture: advertisements in, 102; Bailey and, 15; Boerner and, 74; boundary and fencing elements and, 76; Cranefield and, 49,

70; distribution of, 46; grandmother's gardens and, 88; Hobbins and, 56–57; improvement movement and, 60; March 1913 edition of, *45*; photograph from, *85*; plant recommendations of, 103, 115–119; pleasure gardening and, 51; reader interaction and, 115; recommendations in, 73; rock gardens and, 95, *95*; shrubs and, 124; site planning and, 72; specialty gardens and, 94, *94*; vegetable growing and, 92–93, 122; vine use and, 89; women and, 48; WSHS and, xvii

The Wisconsin Horticulturist: Campbell and, 48; improvement movement and, 60; Manning and, 63; overview of, xvii; "page fences" and, 75; publication of, 45; vegetable gardens and, 91, 92, 122

'Wisconsin Red' dahlia, *114*

Wisconsin State Agricultural Society, 28, 29–30, 44, 62, 74, 79, 90

Wisconsin State Horticultural Society (WSHS): Bailey and, 15; boundary and fencing elements and, 74–79; civic improvement movement and, 49–50; flower bed placement and, 86–88; flower recommendations and, 109–119; history of, xvii, 43–46; home landscape trends recommended by, 51–58; improvement movement and, 60–61; influence of, 42; lawn, path, and driveway appearance and, 79–81; members of, 44, *44*, 45; native plant use and, 95–100; plant recommendations and, 101–104; records and publications of, xvii–xix; rose recommendations and, 119; shrub placement and, 84–86; shrub recommendations and, 107–109; space differentiation and, 61–74; specialty gardens and, 94–95; topics and issues important to, xviii, 46; tree placement and, 81–83; tree recommendations and, 104–106; vegetable garden placement and, 90–93; vegetable gardens and, 122; victory gardens and, 50–51; vine use and, 88–90, 120; women and, 135; women members of, 48, 135

Wisconsin Territory, 26–27

Woman's Club of Madison, 42

women: civic activity of, 20, 42, 50; immigrant gardens and, 39, 41; outdoor activities and, 12; role of, in gardening, xviii, 47; social welfare of, 17; suffrage, xix; Wisconsin Garden Club Federation and, 51; Wisconsin State Horticultural Society and, 48, 135

woodbine, 112, 138

World War I, 50–51

Wychwood, 57–58, *57*

yarrow, *137*

Yawkey House Museum, *117, 130*

'Yellow Rambler' rose, *120*

zinnias, 113

Mrs. Zimmerman of Madison and her window box spilling over
with nasturtiums, geraniums, and *Tradescantia zebrina*, circa 1898